Tales from the Flipside

Mark Devlin

Tales from the Flipside
Mark Devlin

Paperback Edition First Published in Great Britain in 2024
eBook Edition First Published in Great Britain in 2024

Copyright © Mark Devlin 2024

Mark Devlin has asserted his rights under 'the Copyright Designs and Patents Act 1988' to be identified as the author of this work.

All rights reserved.

No part of this document may be reproduced or transmitted in any form or by any means, electronic, mechanical, photocopying, recording, or otherwise, without prior written permission of the Author.

Disclaimer

All reasonable efforts have been made to contact the copyright holders and that anyone who believes their copyright to be infringed is welcome to contact the author.

The views and opinions expressed in this book are entirely those of the author and do not necessarily reflect the opinions, policy or position of aSys Publishing.

ISBN: 978-1-913438-86-9

aSys Publishing
http://www.asys-publishing.co.uk

FOREWORD FROM THE AUTHOR

Though I've become known for my '*Musical Truth*' books and my allegorical novels, there's long been a "forgotten" work lurking away in the background. A skeleton in the cupboard, if you will!

In 2005 I was still working as a full-time club DJ, and was fortunate enough to be travelling the world playing gigs. As I'd also been a magazine writer, I had it in mind to pen a compendium of anecdotes charting the more interesting and outrageous aspects of DJing life, all delivered with wry humour. It seemed to me that there was a gap in the market for such a tome. And so I self-published '*Flipside*,' my first ever book, in January 2007.

At that point in my life, however, I had yet to undergo any kind of conscious awakening. I was still stuck in mainstream ways of thinking, and thought that life was all about clubs, parties, tunes and travel ... and very little else. I hadn't yet twigged that hidden forces controlled the music industry ... and everything else.

This mindset is apparent in the writing, which gives a snapshot of the mental processes and value systems through which I was operating before beginning to "wake up" to great truths about this world. Throughout the chapters I have added new footnotes, giving my thoughts now on what I wrote back then.

If nothing else, I hope it provides a revealing and humorous glimpse into what life as a travelling DJ was like in the early years of the 2000s.

Enjoy.

TALES FROM THE FLIPSIDE

Exploding the myths of the superstar DJ lifestyle.

Being a DJ is the best job in the world.

In what other profession do you get paid well for doing what you genuinely love? What other job allows you to indulge your love of travel – with somebody else footing the bill? You get fame, profile, fans, even groupies. You get offered free drugs and free sex.[1] You get to meet and entertain thousands of people you've never met before. You get to see your name on flyers, posters and billboards all over the world.

Not only that, but is there any other way to make a living where drinking on the job is not only allowed, it's virtually mandatory? Plus you can smoke. Plus you can wear what you want. With the possible exception of being a pop star or a sporting hero, does 'working' really get any better than this? **

---

1. *Not much of either for me in all my years, though!*

So far so good.

But there's a flipside.

A general rule of life seems to be that there's always a price to pay. Besides, if being a DJ was that easy, everyone would be doing it, right?

From playing smoke-filled ghetto spots with only one turntable, to forcibly frogmarching promoters to the nearest cashpoint as your only apparent means of getting paid, the DJing world is never without a story or two to tell.

It's not your average business, and it's certainly not for everyone. One thing's for sure, though. Life as a DJ is never dull.

** (Actually, having written that, I've just been reminded of a little-known fact told to me by Rob Pascoe of Mercury Records. Apparently, there are men in Guam, in the Northern Mariana Islands, whose full-time job is to travel the countryside and deflower young virgins, who pay them for the privilege. Seemingly under Guam law, it is expressly forbidden for virgins to marry. It wouldn't be right to talk about great jobs without giving this at least a mention!)

CHAPTER 1

CRAPPY NEW YEAR

From the ultimate party night to the ultimate farce. Nothing is certain in the volatile world of the DJ.

When you play records for a living, New Year's Eve is a pretty important night. As arguably the ultimate party date in the calendar, everyone's looking for that hot gig. Not only that, but with every nightclub charging double the normal door rate, it means you as a DJ can also charge double your regular rate. Never a bad thing.

By 2003, I was fairly pleased with my NYE track record. I'd found meaningful employment on the previous thirteen December 31sts, and I was all set to enjoy a fourteenth.

It should have been apparent that the dark clouds of fate were gathering in my general direction when my first engagement for the night, a gig in Germany, got cancelled early in the month. Something told me I'd scored the immediate replacement gig at a large, well-known club in Bristol a little too easily. Nevertheless, with an air of naivety akin to that of the average school-leaver, I set off early in the evening ready to fulfil my commitments. Even as late as walking over the threshold of the club at 10pm, the drama that lay in store over the next two hours was not yet apparent.

The sight of the promoter shuffling nervously towards me put me on instant alert. 'Hi Mark, err, how are you?' he enquired sheepishly. 'What's wrong?', I barked back, with no time to waste on pleasantries. 'Well', he ventured cautiously, 'it turns out the club was sold to a new owner in London at midday today, and they've been wanting to stage their own event with their own DJs tonight. But don't worry! I've told them that our event has been booked for weeks, and they have to go with it. Absolutely! Categorically!'[1]

When a promoter tells you not to worry, the night's still going ahead as planned, it's a bit like a dentist telling you not to worry, it's not going to hurt. The first visual suggestion that all was not as it should be came when I arrived at the booth to find a very well-known London garage DJ already playing. There were five people on the dancefloor.

Upon politely enquiring what was going on, (this being my agreed set time), Mr. Big[2] told me he'd been booked that day by the new club owners. When I pointed out that I'd actually been booked to play this spot weeks earlier, he informed me that he didn't know anything about it and didn't particularly care, as he was off to London directly after his set to go and earn some more money.

---

1. Assuming that a "categorical" assurance from a promoter will end up in the 180-degree opposite direction was always the best way to proceed in the clubs game.

2. I can now reveal that the "Mr. Big" DJ in question was DJ Luck of DJ Luck & MC Neat "A Little Bit of Luck" fame.

Tales from the Flipside

My search for the promoter to try and sort out the mess was pointless. He'd long since barricaded himself behind the office door. My attempts at trying to locate a venue manager, deputy manager or janitor-in-chief were equally fruitless. I was on my own in this one.

On a quest for some semblance of sanity, I headed to the front door, looking for someone vaguely in charge. By this point, a magical transformation had taken place. A mammoth queue was stretched around the block, each punter anxiously clutching their ticket for the original promotion, the one I was due to be playing at. Having absorbed the sight, I walked back to the door to get back in. The security gorillas weren't having it. Despite my protestations that I was the DJ, and that these idiots had already seen me go inside once, they refused to let me past.

By this point, a rumble was starting to develop at the pay box. It had become apparent to the first group of punters that the night had been switched without prior notice, and they were now faced with the prospect of a UK garage night, rather than the R&B and hip hop one they'd paid £25 a ticket to attend.

As the discontent spread, Chinese whisper-like, down the line, it was possible to pinpoint the precise moment when the crowd reached its breaking point, and in an act of monumental solidarity, a couple of hundred people instantaneously rushed the door, knocked the bouncers to their feet, and streamed into the club. Some leapt over the pay box and helped themselves to the takings, with no intervention from the terrified till girl to worry about. Others hurled themselves into the coat check and ran off with anything they could grab.

I saw my moment. The only thing on my mind had been the fact that my records, the essential tools of my trade, were still inside the club, so I allowed myself to be swept along in the flow, hot-tailed it to the DJ box where Mr. Big had stopped playing and was looking like a rabbit in the headlights, and scarpered. I just got out before the police on horseback arrived, closely followed by three riot vans, as the street erupted into carnage.

Ten minutes later, I was trundling back along the M4 as the heavens opened and it pissed down. Almost precisely on the stroke of midnight. Happy New Year. What should have been the ultimate party night of the previous twelve months had turned into a total nightmare. No earnings, and a whole heap of hassle. Bet this never happened to Pete Tong.[3]

Not, however, an entirely unique scenario in this particular line of work.

So how the hell did it get to this? And if this is what happens in the DJ game, why do any of us do it?!

*

I was influenced by the pre-credit sequences in the James Bond films in offering this anecdote as the first story. The movies always gave the viewer a tantalising action sequence ahead of the main credits to hook them in. I attempted a variation on the process.

---

3. *I now know why these kinds of things don't happen to the likes of Pete Tong! (See 'Musical Truth Sound Bites.')*

CHAPTER 2
ESCAPE FROM THE MIDDLE OF THE ROAD

'I never thought it would happen, this rap and stuff,
I was too used to packing gats and stuff.'
'Damn right I like the life I live,
'Cos I went from negative to positive,
And it's all good.'

Notorious B.I.G: 'Juicy' (1994)

'Hate it or love it dun, the dog's on top,
And I'm gonna shine homie, 'til my heart stops.
Go ahead, envy me, I'm rap's MVP,
And I ain't going nowhere so you can get to know me.'

The Game Featuring 50 Cent: 'Hate It Or Love It' (2005)

'So if you want to be the best, I'll tell you how,
Put your hand in the air and take the vow:
'I know I can
Be what I want I want to be
If I work hard at it,
I'll be where I want to be'

Nas: 'I Can' (2002)

Mark Devlin

Mediocrity is a ghetto. But music can set you free.

To be taken seriously as a hip hop artist, you have to be from the ghetto. You have to have lived life at the sharp end, and pulled yourself up through all kinds of dramas. It helps if your family was broke, your father was absent, and you sold drugs on the street.[1] All are well-respected hip hop credentials. If you've been shot, that's good—use it. If you're middle to upper class and from the suburbs, either be an R&B singer, or just make sure it never comes out. (Vanilla Ice, anyone?)

In many ways, there are parallels to DJing, albeit less dramatic, particularly if hip hop and its associated genres are your chosen form of music. In the UK, you're already halfway there if you're from London. Otherwise, an upbringing anywhere with a multicultural environment is a good breeding ground. You get exposure to many cross-sections of the community, experience wildly varying lifestyles, and are spoilt for resources when it comes to record shops, bars, clubs and studios. You also tend to get more creative, ambitious, and generally colourful people in larger towns and cities. They're qualities that tend to be cultivated by urban surroundings.

Then there's Witney.

For readers who are unaware, Witney is a small market town in West Oxfordshire, about twelve miles West of Oxford. It's pleasant enough to look at, and handy for the Cotswolds. There's nothing really wrong with it. It's just that, if you have ambitions to make it in the music business, it's pretty much a road to nowhere.

---

1. *It also helps if you were born into the "right" family, or if you made a Faustian bargain with the industry for fame and fortune!*

Tales from the Flipside

As far as I'm aware, no-one from Witney has ever made it remotely big in the music/ entertainment industries...ever.[2] A couple of decades ago, it seemed to be populated almost entirely by middle-of-the-road, middle-class, middle-aged white people. These days, you're more likely to encounter young ASBO-dodging chavs, flitting between rowdy pubs and kebab shops. The Sun, 20 B&H and a pint of Stella. The pubs all play whatever's in the charts. If you're into wet T-shirt contests and karaoke, Witney's a paradise, But it's no place to be if you decide you want to be a 'serious' DJ.

In my own particular random throw of life's dice,[3] I was born in Oxford, then spent the rest of my childhood and teenage years living in the same three-bedroom semi in Witney. I can't lie, my folks were both good parents. I was an only child, and I had a decent upbringing. We were never rich, and with various jobs ranging from a mechanic to a fire extinguisher engineer,[4] my Dad was far from what you'd call a high earner. But we had enough to get by.

We had one holiday a year, sometimes abroad, but usually not. In keeping with the annoying tendency towards compromise that I've shown throughout my life, I went to college but not to university. Yeah, I guess you could say my entire upbringing was one long exercise in mediocrity. There's nothing spectacular, dramatic or profound to say about it. In keeping with everything else in Witney, it was humdrum and absolutely routine.

---

2. Perhaps the only exception to this is my school friend Damien Mendis, the guy who got me into black dance music early on, who has had a moderately successful career as a producer and remixer.

3. Or WAS it really random??

4. My dad having occupied those kinds of jobs, I was NEVER going to make it big in the music game!

The aspect of the whole culture of hip hop that I appreciate and respect the most, is the way that it represents turning negatives into positives. Becoming an MC has saved the lives of countless teenagers from the ghetto—literally. This respectable and relevant art form has enabled them to channel their energy into profitable creativity, rather than let their surroundings send them down the wrong path, to jail or even death. This is the positivity that can come from a hard upbringing.

Now, anyone that's had a tough, broke childhood is going to have difficulty understanding this, but anyone who had an upbringing like mine may be able to relate. In a way, growing up in Witney was a kind of ghetto-isation. In an inner city ghetto, you're deprived of things like decent education, social services and local amenities. In a listless country market town, you're deprived of the buzz and vibrancy of cosmopolitan urban surroundings. This was highly restrictive to my chosen career. Although I never wanted for anything financially, if you get into black urban music, and decide you want to make a living out it, this isn't the most inspiring of surroundings!

Because it's easier than looking for other reasons, I put my relatively late start in the game down to the instant restrictions dumped on me by the place I just happened to be born, and I've always wondered whether my career would have panned out differently if I'd been raised in London. Or Birmingham. Or Bristol. Or anywhere else.

My unwillingness to be associated with Witney can be traced right back to my formative years when I consciously worked on avoiding the local country bumpkin twang that characterised the area. My self-imposed elocution lessons succeeded in losing the local accent, even if the resulting hybrid[5] now seems to confuse people into thinking I'm either from London, or, bizarrely, Australia?? Not quite sure what happened there.

There were no black or Asian people in Witney in the 70s. It was the sort of place where kids would refer to 'wogs' and 'pakis', even though they'd never met one. There were two Chinese kids in my school, though. The other kids used call the girl names, but they knew better than do it to to the boy, 'cause he was hard and did that kung fu shit.

You might wonder how anyone so sheltered from cosmopolitanism could ever get into hip hop and R&B.

One thing for which I'll always be grateful to my Mum was having the radio on in the house. When I was a kid, it was hardly ever off. Okay, we're talking Terry Wogan on Radio 2 here, and the music rarely got any more hardcore than Abba. But humble beginnings are good. And the thing that really got me started was the fact that the set was switched to Radio 1 at 5pm on a Sunday, which meant I got a weekly exposure to the Top 40—two whole hours of contemporary pop music implanted firmly into my impressionable brain!

Now, this was useful, because besides the blandness of Abba, it meant I also got to hear the soul and disco of the 70s, the New Wave, Two Tone and New Romantic hits of the early 80s, and assorted other good stuff. And the effect was so profound that I went out and bought my first record when I was five. I think it cost about 35p from Woolworths.

---

5. *What my family has long described as my "radio voice"...which has served me pretty well in the career path I've ended up in, as it turns out!*

Most people have to either cringe or lie when they reveal their first record, because it was something wack like The Wombles. In my case, I can hold my head up and say with dignity that it was Queen's 'Bohemian Rhapsody' during its original nine-week reign at number one. Sure, it would have been cooler if it was Barry White or Stevie Wonder, but most people respect 'Bo Rhap.' (My first album was the 'Grease' soundtrack, which helps redress the credibility balance a little.)

I quickly discovered I had a pretty amazing memory for music, and even now, I can hear tunes from the 70s and early 80s, and not only be able to name the artist, title, record label and chart position, (that makes me a trainspotter, right?), I can also recall in intricate detail exactly where I was at when I first heard them.

A friend once bet me 50p I couldn't recall and recite Gary Byrd's entire 10-minute, 35-second rap on 'The Crown'.

He lost.

There's not much that was 'gangsta' about my early life, but at least I can say I hated school. Because I was skinny, quiet and shy, most of the other kids hated me, so it was easy to hate 'em back. The only positive thing to come out of this was that it built up my resilience and independence, and started me on the path of doing things for myself without having to rely on other people—something that's worked for me ever since. Is there any other way?

There have been half a dozen hugely influential people in my life, to the degree that my subsequent career is likely to have been radically different if we'd never met. He might not realise it, but the first of these was a guy called Damien Mendis, the sole Asian kid in my school during my teenage years. He went on to be a highly successful record producer, working in New York and LA with artists like Brandy and

Janet Jackson, and we sadly lost contact. But we became friends when we were 15, largely as a result of being marginalised by other kids, though moreso by blatantly showing that we didn't give a shit either way.

We started bringing our radio cassettes in on Tuesday lunchtimes, the time when Gary Davies[6] announced the week's brand new top 40 on Radio 1, and we'd have hordes of other kids crowding around us, Pied Piper-like, desperate to find out what was number one. We were popular then. In the Land of the Mundane, the kid with the ghetto blaster is King.

While everyone else our age was going into their gothic phase, lapping up The Smiths and The Cure, Damien was into the 'black' music of the day. We're talking stuff like Jimmy Jam and Terry Lewis' productions on Janet Jackson, The SOS Band and Alexander O' Neal, and pop-soul like Princess, The Cool Notes and Loose Ends. Cameo were big, too, Larry Blackmon the subject of hysteria in our class with his absurdly overstated red codpiece, and they ended up being the first act I ever saw live. Damien used to bring a radio cassette into art lessons, and I was far more interested in the tapes he'd made at home than the drawing. Once, I remember a kid screwing up his face and asking, 'how come all the stuff you listen to is by black people?' 'Because they make the best music,' Damien replied. A simple truth.

It was the first time I'd heard all this stuff, and something about being into it appealed to my going-against-convention mentality. Plus the fact, as Damien had pointed out, that it was damn fine music. It was a good time to

---

6. These days it's hard to name any Radio1 DJ from back in the day who's NOT been embroiled in some kind of sex scandal or other, but I've never heard any such accusations directed at Gary Davies.

be open-minded, as hip hop was just going into its most creative phase. At the tail end of 1985, Doug E Fresh's 'The Show' was released, and it was a record that changed my whole attitude to music. When I first heard it, like everyone else at school, I thought it was ridiculous, Slick Rick's nonsensical storytelling, and crazy 'Inspector Gadget' samples over a mad shuffling beat. But the more I listened, the more I started to appreciate just how original and groundbreaking it was, and it taught me to judge a record on the very essence of how it sounds, rather than what category it might fall into—or whether everyone else likes it.

After this, things like Whistle's 'Just Buggin' came out, equally 'ridiculous', but more easily appreciated after 'The Show'. Robbie Vincent's 'Sound Of Sunday Nite' was the mandatory radio listening, and James Hamilton's weekly column in Record Mirror was revered like a religious document. Then, it was Def Jam's finest hour, with the likes of LL Cool J, Run DMC, EPMD, and later, Public Enemy all starting to emerge. By the time I heard 'Rebel Without A Pause', I was a fully-fledged hip hop head.

One thing for which I do count myself lucky was being born when I was. It meant that by the late 80s, I was of just the right age to appreciate the phenomenal changes that were going on in black/ urban/ dance music. These days, everything is neatly confined to categories—there's a techno 'scene', a house 'scene', an R&B 'scene', a drum 'n' bass 'scene', etc, each with its own discernible sound, image, lifestyle and fanbase, and very little crossover between. Stick a hardcore hip hop head in a trance club full of sweating, glowstick-waving ravers and watch him grimace. Or do the opposite, and watch him crap himself!

But from 1986 to '90, it was all one big melting pot. House music in its very earliest form was starting to cross over from Chicago and Detroit, and it was adopted by the soul and funk fans of the day, as it was another strand of underground black music that wasn't yet ready for the mainstream. These were the days when Paul Oakenfold, Pete Tong,[7] Danny Rampling and co. used to play black music, (before the enticement of big bucks led them, trance-like towards the mass-market dance scene), and when it was nothing unusual to hear Steve 'Silk' Hurley's 'Jack Your Body' or Inner City's 'Big Fun' played alongside Eric B and Rakim's 'I Know You Got Soul', or Oran 'Juice' Jones' 'The Rain' . . . by the same DJ! When I first started going to clubs, (underage, of course. I was a rebel by now!), this is how it was. Then it was '88 and the era of acid house . . . and there's enough books out there about this particular story to avoid me needing to repeat it.

Although I was well on the road to my music-dominated outlook by now, my clubbing experiences were still pretty lame. I can't claim to have enjoyed acid nights at Shoom or Spectrum. Me and Damien were restricted to a student night called Lust at Boodles in Oxford on a Monday, or general-purpose Saturdays at The Coven or Downtown Manhattan, where if you were really lucky, the DJ might drop 'We Call It Acieeed' between Yazz and Milli Vanilli. I went to The Wag in London once that year, though, and I felt like the coolest motherfucker on the planet.

In fact, at that stage, it looked very much as if I might go down the house music route myself.[8] What set me on the alternative course for good, like so many other DJs in the UK, was listening to Tim Westwood. This was in the days of the legendary Capital Rap Show, long before his

---

7. *See my contemporary "exposes" of Tong and Oakenfold—plus a few other "gatekeepers" in 'Musical Truth Sound Bites'!*

8. *I wish I had now, given my more recent discoveries about long-hidden secrets within hip-hop!*

departure to Radio One. It was in the days when Westwood didn't shout and scream and tell jokes. He just played serious, underground, undiluted hip hop, laced with the ragga and swing of the day. The production was impeccable. It was pure drama, and the show ended up captivating me. I'd never heard stuff like this before, (in Witney?!) and I quickly got caught up in the whole idea of hip hop and its associated genres.

The main appeal was that hip hop encompassed not just a style of music, but a whole way of life. It has its own language, clothing, cars, movies, food, and overall lifestyle[9] that just can't be matched by any other genre. Call me philosophical, but the original ethos of hip hop, the idea that kids from the street with nothing can elevate themselves to a higher level through this original and creative art form, really appealed to me as well. So I was hooked, and it was clear that rap, ragga and swing (as it used to be called,) was the music for me.

Although I was carrying myself with a certain air of exclusivity that stated I was now into far better stuff than anyone else, (and I can tell you any other DJ out there has conceitedly believed this at one time or another!) there was no getting away from the truth. I was still a wannabe.

And they can be a real pain in the ass!

---

9. I clearly had zero understanding of the science of social-engineering at this point!

CHAPTER 3

SOMEWHERE TO RUN

'Bout to retire, pull a Hova.
I quit. No more. It's over for Jin.
I'm tired, that's it!'

Jin: 'I Quit' (2005)

Before you become a DJ, it pays to consider what you'll do when it all dries up![1]

By the time I was 18, I knew I wanted to be a DJ. Music was my one passion in life, and I could think of nothing better than making a living out of sharing my tastes in it with other people, and trying to make them appreciate it as much as I did.

Only one problem. I had absolutely no idea how to go about it. So I took the easy option, and didn't bother. I just carried on working in Waitrose. For two years. On the Deli counter.[2] It was the ultimate cop-out, and I've

---

1. *I think I've pretty much managed to get myself sorted in that regard ... not that it was ever part of any plan!*

2. *The major contributing factor in my becoming a vegetarian when I'd seen a thing or two about how meat is prepared for sale.*

cursed myself for my early inactivity ever since—although I was hardly the first 18-year-old to take a bit longer than necessary to get away from the starting block!

Let's be honest, though. Being a DJ is basically frowned upon as a career choice. Show me a school, college, careers office or parent that will recommend it as a respectable and reliable profession. Everyone thinks you'll do drugs and fall in with a bad crowd. And rolling in at dawn will always get you frowns and comments like 'when are you going to get a proper job?'

But it's only fair to look at the flipside, and there are many admirable elements to this line of work which are hard to contest. As a DJ, you can operate as a self-employed business, which brings responsibility and independence. There are endless creative options, such as making your own music, running your own events, maintaining your own promotional website...and creativity is good for the mind. And if you're really successful, you can actually make far more money than 'respectable' professions like a lawyer, doctor or bank manager! All without going to university, too—something you may find is considered more of a hindrance than a help in this game. Do you think Judge Jules has any regrets about graduating from law school, then deviating totally and following the path of a DJ? Or does Tim Westwood lament flunking all his exams at public school? Somehow I doubt it.[3]

Anyway, by the age of 20, life on the nightshift at Tesco was doing my head in, the possible sole benefit being that it climatised my body for the forthcoming onslaught of a nocturnal lifestyle. But I don't feel too bitter about it now since learning that Danny Rampling used to be a milkman

---

3. *Again, see 'Musical Truth Sound Bites' for more on how I see these two—and many of their contemporaries—now!*

and postman, Carl Cox was a scaffolder, (before becoming a champion disco dancer!), Graeme Park was a pea-packer, and Sasha worked in a fish factory.

Feeling the pressure to follow a sensible job course, I decided the thing to do was to pursue a career in journalism. I'd always enjoyed expressing myself in writing, and considered I was pretty good at it. Plus, I figured I could use it to start writing about music, only one step away from actually playing it.

When it comes to anecdotal cliches, 'being in the right place at the right time' is a perennial favourite. Although the opposite is something with I'm far more familiar, in 1991, I was amazed to find that Witney actually offered a fantastic job opportunity, only five minutes from my front door.

A business-to-business publishing house called Trade Media Ltd. needed a reporter to work on its flagship magazine. They were happy to take on a complete novice and train them from scratch in all aspects of magazine writing. The subject matter wasn't ideal—it was stationery and office supplies. But it didn't matter. This was the perfect way to learn the art of writing. Plus there was the additional challenge of making the content sound lively. If you can do it with pencil sharpeners, you can do it with anything.

It was a great opportunity to cut corners and make up some lost time, too, because within a year I'd made Assistant Editor, within another, Deputy Editor, and by 1994 at the age of 24, I was Editor of my own magazine, and it had all been achieved without any formal, recognised training or qualifications—only immense hard work. Just goes to show, the only way to really get qualified for a job is to just get stuck in and start learning at the sharp end.

Anyway, through all this time, my aspirations to become a DJ never waned. But I realised that what was emerging was a very effective plan B, a safety-net infrastructure that should be set in place before going any further.

In the volatile, fickle and unpredictable world of club DJing, a plan B is an essential requirement. It's the first piece of advice I'd give to any aspiring young novice, and I'm astounded by the amount of successful DJs that seemingly give no thought to where they're going to run when it all dries up.

DJing has a sell-by date. Although there are exceptions like Bob Jones, Graham Gold, David Rodigan, Pete Tong and Tim Westwood, who are all still DJing at the wrong side of 45,[4] for the most part, it's not a job you still want to be doing when the flab starts to spread and the hair starts to thin.

It's always been my plan to retire gracefully before the embarrassment point, and settle back into journalism as a way of carrying me through the rest of my working years. There's no shame in being a 60-year-old writer.[5]

The Plan B logic's plain enough, but so many DJs seem to miss it. The prime example of this was when the bubble finally burst on the UK garage scene towards the end of 2001. Clubland violence, mis-management, exploitation and burn-out caused by the music peaking too high too soon, threw up countless casualties who'd been racing round the country doing four gigs a night and earning stupid money one minute, only to become confused and disillusioned and wondering why their wallets were empty the next. The result was that many tried to 'reinvent' themselves as R&B DJs and leap on

---

4. And now, in most cases, into their 60s and beyond!

5. ...which is good, because it's about all I have left!

board that scene to stay alive. This was after a couple of years of arrogantly rejecting it in favour of their own movement.

Then you have R&B DJs who have become house DJs overnight, swearing they were always into it, purely because they can't get the work any more.[6] And vice-versa.

The smart DJs are the most successful ones, and they're the ones that have another string to their bow. Rightly or wrongly, it's not enough to just be a hot DJ that can rock a crowd. It's a marketing-driven game, and you have to have some kind of brand or organisation that you're associated with in order to make it big. You need to work for a label, like Matt White at Polydor, or you need to make music, like Dodge. If you win a MOBO Award like Manny Norte or Shortee Blitz, you're laughing, as that'll keep you at the top of your game for at least a couple of years, (and double your fee).

The most reliable catalyst is to have a radio show. Steve Sutherland, DJ Swerve, Semtex, Rampage and Steve Wren will tell you that. (Trevor Nelson will tell you it helps to be on TV, too—whether it's a music show, a car show, a travel show, a 'reality TV' show, a game show, etc, etc, etc . . .)[7] You can be a promoter and put on your own jams, and you may well make some money. But the risks

---

6. I'm guilty of making that switch in more recent years, but not to pursue the riches. I simply no longer enjoy what now passes as "hip-hop" but still have a lot of love for the more soulful side of house music.

7. Trevor is now an MBE, as are Jazzie B, Norman Jay and David Rodigan, so they've all ingratiated themselves to the system in some way.

involved are the same as being a DJ, and your sell-by date is similar.

The house/ dance scene, as with so many other aspects, is much better organised on this one. Virtually all the big names on that side have remix/ production skills to their name, or a record label, or a management company, or something.

In my case, being associated with Blues & Soul, the long-running and market-leading urban music magazine, has clearly been responsible for over 50 per cent of my bookings over the past few years. Editing and subbing the entire UK and Ireland club listings section has put me in an unbeatable position when it comes to keeping up with what nights are happening where, and who the most active promoters are.

The critics are right when they opine that club DJing is not a secure profession. Like acting and pop music, the nightlife world is vicious, savage and heartless.[8] You can be snowed under with work one minute, and queuing at the Job Centre the next. (The same goes for pop stars—where are Nik Kershaw, Limahl and Chesney Hawkes now, eh?!)

I've known countless casualties who've had to go back to dead-end day jobs when their DJing world has crumbled. They've been devastated that their dream has flopped, but it can happen any minute, and it wouldn't have been half as hard to bear if they'd had something else to fall back on when it did.

I eventually realised my dream, overcame all fears and obstacles and became a DJ, of course—hence this book! After much deliberation, however, I always resisted

---

8. *I was right, but mistaken in assuming that this dynamic applied ONLY to the music world!*

adopting a DJ stage name, as so many other jocks do. I wanted there to be no confusion about who I was, and as my own name kinda sounded like a DJ name anyway, I stuck with it. (Although my Dad's ahead of me here; his initials are actually D.J Devlin.)[9]

The most popular type of specific DJ moniker, of course, is simply to call yourself DJ such-and-such, Excalibah, Swerve and Spoony being good examples. (Helps throw the taxman off the scent, of course . . . not that I'm suggesting that any of these fellas indulge in such behaviour, of course!) It's surprising how much you think of these people by their DJ names after a while, too. I always greet One Step with a 'wattup Step', rather than a 'hello, Tony.' (Along similar lines I called DJ Sugarman from Coventry 'Sugar' a couple of times, before I realised my mistake.)

That's fair enough. But the thing that's always struck me as a little unimaginative is when jocks simply call themselves DJ Dave, or DJ Sammy, or DJ whatever-their-real-name-happens-to-be. It's like other parts of society calling themselves Bank Manager Jeremy, or Truck Driver Keith, or Cleaning Lady Doreen. It just wouldn't happen, would it?[10]

---

9. *These days I get accused of my name being coded—"Mark of the Devil." "I TOLD you he was a satanist! For the record, the name Devlin is actually an Anglicisation of the original Gaelic "O'Diobhlain" where the "bh" is pronounced as "v." Not much "devilish" about that.*

10. *Similarly "Freemason" or "intel agent" such-and-such wouldn't really work either!*

CHAPTER 4
WHAT'S THE DIFFERENCE?

'What's the difference between me and you?
About five bank accounts, three ounces and two vehicles.'

Dr. Dre Featuring Xzibit: 'What's The Difference?' (1999)

'I remember when I couldn't even afford a Ford Escort.'

Kanye West:' Diamonds' (2005)

'OK gang, it's checkout time for yours truly.
Boy, I love you, I love y'all, but I gotta go,
The Rolls is double-parked downstairs,
Suit's in the cleaners and I gotta get my diamonds clean.
It's the weekend and I'm going out for some action, you know what I mean?'

The Concept: 'Mr. DJ' (1986)

'From the sharks in the penthouse to the rats in the basement,
It's not that far.'

Kirsty MacColl: 'Walking Down Madison' (1991)

Tales from the Flipside

There's a gulf between the different types of DJ...in money, respect, and airline check-in procedures.[1]

Up to now, you've heard all about DJs as a collective breed. But, as with pimps, porn stars and politicians, there are many different types of DJ, all with distinct differences in approach, profile, lifestyle,...and financial success.[2]

Categorising them broadly, they can split into three sub-groups, and the most abundant is your common-or-garden general-purpose DJ. This is the guy who drives around in a van marked 'Dave's Mobile Disco—Weddings, Private Functions, etc'. He may well just spin at weekends, perhaps working as a plasterer or plumber during the week. He may well be middle-aged, balding, and boast an impressive beer gut. He's happy to play anything from Frank Sinatra to Aqua, as circumstances dictate, and he does alright for himself as a result.

Next up is the house/ dance music DJ, and this is the character most people think of when they hear the term 'superstar DJ', because they're the only ones that have any kind of public image. This group includes the likes of Sasha, Pete Tong, Carl Cox and Paul Oakenfold, (notable for having been assessed as 'the world's most successful DJ' by the Guinness Book of Records a few years ago.)[3] It also includes Norman Cook/ Fatboy Slim, who holds the distinction of being the only DJ apart from me that my Mum has ever heard of. (Although she occasionally makes veiled references to Tim Westwood as 'that bloke who got

---

1. And also in terms of allotted Lifetime Actors, it now turns out!

2. And family bloodline backgrounds.

3. See 'Musical Truth Sound Bites'!

shot—you know.') On top of that, it's the only category where there's a reasonably healthy abundance of female DJs, the likes of Lisa Lashes, Anne Savage and Sister Bliss leading the pack.

The attractiveness of this genre can be seen by the handful of washed-up celebs who've turned to the glam world of DJing when their prior careers have started to dry up; Boy George, Nigel Benn and Neneh Cherry are among their numbers. Even Beckham's had a go, God help us!

It's an international set-up, too; besides the UK frontrunners, European giants like Paul Van Dyk, Tiesto, Armin Van Burren, Timo Maas and Ferry Corsten enjoy phenomenal worldwide success, as do Stateside players like Dave Morales, Roger Sanchez, Erick Morillo, Danny Tenaglia and Tony Humphries.[4] Yes, it's a far cry from a wedding reception at the back of the Dog and Duck with cheese puffs and sausage rolls all round, or that school disco you remember, with everyone trying to get a slow dance and a snog before Spandau Ballet's 'True' runs out.

The third group is the one I opted to belong to—the specialist DJ—in my case, dealing with hip hop, R&B, soul and reggae, all neatly summed up by the catch-all terms 'black' or 'urban' music.

What's often forgotten—or never known—is that virtually all the UK DJs now considered pioneers of house or 'dance' music, started out in just this way. In the 80s, if you weren't a pop jock, the only alternative was soul, funk and early hip hop. Pete Tong was a big name on the South East's 'soul mafia' scene, alongside much older players like Chris Hill, Greg Edwards and Jeff Young. Judge Jules played rare groove at warehouse parties, alongside the likes of Norman Jay and Soul II Soul. Graham Gold,

---

4. *And now, with the benefit of hindsight and the ability to do independent research, we have some clues as to why!*

Carl Cox and Danny Rampling were soul DJs; Paul Oakenfold ran the UK offices of hip hop labels Def Jam and Profile. Unbelievably, Dave Pearce was a hip hop head, too, becoming the first UK DJ to interview Public Enemy. What happened, Dave?![5]

(There are other genres of DJ, of course—acid jazz/ eclectic dudes like Gilles Peterson or Patrick Forge, indie characters like Zane Lowe, and the whole drum 'n' bass crowd like Fabio and Grooverider. There's also the surreal world of Northern soul, about which countless books have been written and a world unto itself, but for the sake of simplicity, we'll leave them out of this!)

Anyway, far from being one big happy family, there's actually very little fraternising between the sub-groups. Many dance DJs I know regard urban jocks as an unimportant sub-breed several notches below them in the food chain. Urban DJs, similarly, tend to view most dance jocks as spoilt, overpaid, pill-popping prima donnas. And possibly gay.

The truth is, the lifestyles attached to each genre are so radically different, that it's more a cultural, anthropological gap than a musical one. As a result, it's struck me for years that there's an immense, insurmountable gulf between the fortunes of house DJs and those of urban DJs like myself. Here's just three ways in which it manifests itself.

Opportunities

Of the three, it's plain to see that the (successful) dance/ house DJ enjoys a far better quality of existence than the others. First of all, house music became a global[6]

---

5. See 'Musical Truth Sound Bites'!

6. *I no longer use this word!*

movement years ago. Although R&B has now gone the same way, house got there first, and is now understood by legions of dedicated followers on every continent. This means there are far more opportunities available, in clubs, in radio, even in press coverage. The only hip hop DJ to ever make the UK national press is Tim Westwood, and he had to get shot to achieve it.[7]

When it comes to club nights, the house scene has it all neatly sewn-up, and UK promoters have been at the pinnacle of this international phenomenon for years. Pioneering clubs like Cream, Gatecrasher, Ministry of Sound and God's Kitchen have gone on to become hugely marketable brands, spawning tours, Summer festivals, compilation albums, radio shows, clothing lines and much more. It's hard to think of many other industries which have bred such entrepreneurialism in the last two decades.

Some find this surprising. House promoters are usually thought of in terms of their high-resistance threshold when it comes to shovelling copious amounts of narcotics into their system, and logic suggests they should end up broke and in rehab. But they get the job done. Not only that, but they make shedloads out of it, too!

So, how does the R&B scene compete? Generally with a never-ending glut of nights promoted on Identikit glossy flyers with pictures of J-Lo's ass, or some generic beenie in a bikini. If they last a year they're lucky. The only UK R&B night that's ever been promoted to the same degree of success as the top-league house nights is Smoove, for five years the top urban night out on a Friday, (now relegated to monthly Sundays.) Little surprise that it's the product of the world-famous dance club Ministry of Sound.

To be fair, though, the urban music world does have a whole host of obstacles to overcome. If there's the slightest

---

7. *Well, not JUST that!*

hint of trouble, many local police forces are quick to make the venue shut a night down, with the heavy-handed suggestion that it doesn't stage any more 'black' music events in the future. This happened a few years ago in Manchester when gangland feuds were rife, to the extent that the city's nightlife was virtually destroyed. (Happily it's back again now.) It happened again in Birmingham in early 2003, in the wake of the New Year's Day drive-by killing of two girls outside a Handsworth nightspot. And the recent riots sparked by a pirate DJ's comments about a supposed rape have had the same regressive effect.

Locations where urban music nights are going to work are limited, too. By comparison to house, R&B is steeped in all kinds of cultural influences, so tends to be more of an acquired taste, or part of a lifestyle. Inevitably, openings are going to be limited on this basis, and largely restricted to urban areas with multicultural populations. Not much R&B action in Northumberland.

Our friend Dave, of course, doesn't have to worry. It's like supermarkets; as long as people eat food, they'll always be in business. As long as people want to go out get pissed and have a good singalong, and pull,—and, possibly, a curry and a fight on the way home—Dave's putting food on his table!

Money

Maybe this is the real reason why urban DJs harbour such resentment towards their dance music cousins? While the average (non-famous) R&B DJ might be lucky to pick up £200 for a night's work, there's the knowledge that the average fourth league house DJ could easily be earning five times the amount for the same set.

Turn your head to the sky and you might even see Sasha's private jet returning him home, easily funded by the ten grand he's just picked up for his own two-hour shift. (The dance music world even started questioning itself around the time of Millennium Night, 1999. There were allegations of headline DJs picking up £100,000 for one night's work!)

Getting paid can be an adventure in itself at urban music jams. There are very few contracts or deposit payments. It's all about cash. I once did about six gigs in a row for a very well-known club in Bristol, which in fact, is little more than a dimly-lit warehouse on the edge of the ghetto. At the end of each night, I was led along a network of underground passages to a dungeon-like office, a bit like the pit in 'Silence Of The Lambs', where no-one would hear you scream. It was full of unsavoury characters, and each time I was convinced I wouldn't leave with both kneecaps intact. Miraculously, not only did I survive, I left every session fully paid up—even if one time it was entirely in pound coins, stuffed into two butchers' carrier bags![8]

Another time, at another venue, two of the notes in the crumpled wad I was handed were smeared in what was clearly fresh blood. No sign of any sweat or tears.

One of the biggest mistakes made by those outside the profession, is to automatically assume promoters in London pay the best. Wrong.

They may well charge more at the door than the cost of the average Ryanair flight to Europe; their drinks prices may well be a revelation...of what other venues will be charging in around ten years; and you may well be able to buy an entire can of Lynx for the two quid the guy in the toilets expects for the single spray he's just given you, but trust me, London promoters have the tightest wallets in

---

8. *I can now reveal this was the venue Lakota!*

clubland. DJ fees in the capital are a joke, which is why you see so many London DJs fleeing town every weekend to go and earn some proper money elsewhere!

On top of that, many of them employ the outrageous tactic of paying DJs according to their ability to bring their mates to the club. So if twenty people turn up on the direct recommendation of the DJ, he might get £5 of their £15 door fee. The promoter gets £10, and the venue scoops up the remaining £20 each that they spend at the bar!

The tactic London promoters use is an extension of the 'if you don't want to do it, there's hundreds of others out there who will' theory. It's to simply play one DJ off against the next. Gigs end up being an auction, ultimately going to the DJ charging the lowest fee.

London venues need to learn a trick or two about hospitality, too. It's nothing unusual not to be offered a drink all night, and if you finally have the gall to ask for even a bottle of water, you can watch the promoter visibly wince at the thought of having to shell out. (One-time So Solid Crew member Lisa Maffia took pity on my girlfriend and I in one club when the promoter had spent all night fawning over her and had completely ignored me in the process, by sharing her complimentary bottle of champagne with us. Respect!)

Contrast this with gigs in Scotland or Ireland, both famous for their hearty welcomes. If the promoter asks you what you're drinking, he doesn't just mean right now, he means what are you drinking *all night?!* Answer beer, and you get a crate. Answer vodka, and you get a bottle. Now, *that's* how it should be done!

Weight

Urban music DJs tend to carry a lot more weight than their dance music counterparts. It's not a reference to personal fitness, or their standing in the community. It's all down to the weight of their wares.

House/ trance/ techno sessions are all about building vibes and moods, and many DJs will go on about how they 'take you on a journey'. Consequently, any dance records are specifically made with this in mind, and as a result, many tend to be long...very long. The main culprits are the progressive and deep house genres, where it's nothing unusual to get a ten or twelve-minute dub taking up one side of vinyl. Any DJ playing it has enough time to go to the toilet, order a round of drinks, consume at least two, collect a couple of phone numbers, chat to a couple of friends, and return to the booth with still enough time to select and mix in the next tune.

Contrast this with the plight of the urban DJ. Hip hop/ R&B crowds tend to have a lower attention span than house crowds, which means they appreciate fast-moving sets. A DJ responding to this might find himself changing records every minute and a half, cutting after just one verse and chorus, chopping in the next tune at just the right point to bring cheers of appreciation from the crowd.

This has serious implications on the number of records taken to a gig, (assuming the DJ still plays off vinyl, of course, a subject which surely deserves a chapter of its own...see chapter 7!) To fill a three-hour set, an urban DJ might well need two fully-laden metal cases, holding 100 records each. As anyone who's handled this amount of records will tell you, vinyl is not light! Just one of these crates weighs well in excess of 20 kilos. This alone is enough to put you over the personal baggage limit on many airlines, bringing an excess charge.[9]

The dance DJ, meanwhile, might only need 30 tunes to fill his three hours. These can easily be carried in a shoulder bag, and quite happily taken on a plane as hand luggage. Also, many dance DJs have now taken to playing entire sets off CD, something that just couldn't happen in the hip hop world, where you're not taken seriously if you're not spinning slabs of plastic. So not only does the dance DJ get paid more, and get to travel more, he also stands a chance of not giving himself a hernia every time he loads up for a gig!

The airline baggage limits issue is, however, one that can be overcome with a few simple strategies. So here, for the first time in print, are a few of my tips on how to get it right.

1. Firstly, if male, when approaching check-in, always go for the desk with the youngest, meekest looking girl. Chances are she's fairly new to the job, so she won't want the confrontation of challenging you if you happen to be slightly over. Alternatively, just flirt. Never, on any account, go for the stone-faced middle-aged hag who's clearly been in the job twenty years too long, and looks like she's going through a divorce. She'll have you!

(If you're female, just go for the desk with the token male and hope he's not gay!)

2. If the above options don't work, try distracting the agent at the precise moment you put your case on the scales. Ask some dumbfounding question like 'are there Indo-Chino-lacto vegetarian meals on board?', and the chances are they'll be too flummoxed to notice you're ten kilos over.

---

9. *And now all of this music can be fitted on to one tiny USB stick. The digital revolution does have SOME benefits!*

3. Otherwise, here's an absolute belter. If you know you're over-limit, stick a whole load of stuff temporarily in your hand baggage, so your case comes in under-weight. Then, ask to put your luggage on the oversize belt, specially reserved for fragile or bulky items. You generally take your case there yourself, so before you do, find a quiet corner and just put all your stuff straight back in the case. You're through!)

Postscript. In 2004, as if in Heaven-sent response the above, Easyjet announced that they were eliminating weight restrictions on their hand baggage. As long as you could safely lift your luggage into the overhead bins without assistance, you were on. The original DJ-friendly airline!

*

So with the successful dance music DJs playing at well-managed, high profile events, travelling the world in private jets and limos and getting paid well for the privilege, enjoying further promotion through the switched-on dance music press like Mixmag and DJ—and with Dave doing alright for himself, too... why would anyone want to become an R&B or hip hop DJ? There are fewer openings, the competition is fierce, jealousy is rife, club nights are prone to bad organisation and frequent cancellations, and the money's never as good.

Ask any urban music DJ the question, and they'll give you the same answer. It's all down to a love and a genuine passion for the music. If you get into R&B or hip hop in the first place, chances are it's because it speaks to you and has meaning in your life. You live and breathe it, and nothing else will do.

And this is powerful enough to surpass any obstacles. It has to be.

CHAPTER 5

THE HUMAN JUKEBOX

'Now, Mr DJ. I've asked you three times already...Play my muthaf*cking song!

Jennifer Lopez: 'Play' (2002)

A DJ's job would be all plain sailing if it weren't for the punters.

By now, the lay reader will have gathered that unless you're Paul Oakenfold or Jazzy Jeff, the everyday routines of the average honest, hard-working DJ is not without its challenges. By the end of this book, doormen, pissheads, dodgy promoters, haters, goldiggers and the police will all have been taken to task.

There's one other breed whose actions need addressing, however, because they have the potential to be the source of more exasperation and premature grey hair-inducing frustration than any of the other breeds put together.

Punters wanting requests.

Now, this is a difficult one because we, as DJs, really should respect our punters. After all, it's their door tax that pays our fees. And for the most part, punters are great. If you've got a good, responsive crowd, it can give you a great buzz and send you home with a smile on your face, remembering just why you wanted to do this job in the first place.

But the issue of requests involves some of the dumbest scenarios any working DJ is ever going to encounter. And if you're in any doubt as to the passionate feeling this tends to bring about, check out a couple of my favourite posts to the chat forum topic on the subject, which ran recently on my website.

DJ Bobby Speed from Bristol:

'Don't even get me started on requests. Too late. Why is it that women get so arsey and are generally bloody rude when you don't have their tune? Goddam women just get on my nerves! Are we DJs or robots? Are there so many bad DJs out there that we are no longer trusted to choose the records ourselves?

Some guy asked me last night if I took requests. 'No,' I said. 'Why not?' 'Because I don't need to. I know exactly what you, (the crowd,) are going to ask for. 'What's that?', he asked. 'All the shit we hear on the radio, and all the worst tunes I have in my box," I replied. (Yes, sometimes I really am that rude).'[1]

This met with an immediate message of solidarity from Steve Limmer, aka Belfast's Finest. (Parental Advisory warning applies):

'Mr. Speed, you and me are on the same wavelength. I can be a nasty c**t to some of my punters, and I'm impatient with daft song requests. Some punters are thick as shite, and the ignorant ones really get to me!

I can't see any pros in doing requests any more. The club scene has changed so much that the crowds just want to

---

1. *This dynamic, moreso than any other, is what led to me giving up 20 years of full-time DJing in 2014. Enough is enough!*

hear the pop hits, ('hits' being an anagram), so I don't feel that I need the input.

But my personal favourite request, (and this usually crops up when Uni starts first semester,) is the Tupac Boy—you know, the moronic country bumpkin who is hip hop's biggest fan...as long as Dr. Dre produced it. 'You f**kin better play 'California Love'. Grrr.

I'm short-tempered, and the temptation to dish out slaps to these muppets is getting closer by the set.'

(I should point out that I know both Bobby and Belfast's personally, and they've always struck me as cool, regular, balanced, non-chauvinistic guys. The uncharacteristic tone of their comments should help illustrate the levels of frustration we're dealing with here.)

The core problem seems to arise from the way many clubgoers see a DJ's role. To them, the DJ is nothing but a human jukebox, there to cater for their every musical whim, and to play any tune they ask for—from Elvis Presley to Mylo—regardless of what type of club night it happens to be. Within the next five minutes. This is wrong.

On the other hand, what doesn't help is that there are many DJs who totally disregard their crowd, and take the view that they're damn well going to play what they like and you can take it or leave it. These characters can often be seen frowning sullenly with their head tilted downwards. Another way to identify them is by their empty dancefloors.

As I see it, the true art of DJing falls somewhere in the middle. It's a compromise between taking notice of what people are asking for, and maintaining a degree of innovation by playing stuff they really want to get across. If all DJs are going to do is churn out the same old hits that people get on the radio or on MTV's playlist, then we might as well be replaced by machines. It's a DJ's responsibility to introduce music that people might not have heard before, at least some of the time.

(This can be a maddening experience in itself, though. I clearly remember hammering Beyonce's 'Crazy In Love' the first week it came out. Because nobody had heard it before, they just stood around with their arms folded, or left the dancefloor. A month later, it was the biggest R&B/pop crossover hit of the decade, and it was receiving 20 requests an hour. *It was exactly the same piece of music they were listening to!* Why wouldn't they trust my judgement and respond to it in the first place! Grrrr.)

Anyway, there are several different types of requesting punters, and here are a few scenarios which, I guarantee you, will be familiar to every working DJ on the planet.

The worst possible variety is the punter who thinks it's their job to tell the DJ what to play. You get them everywhere.

A lot of the more moody, 'serious' DJs, particularly on the house scene, prefer to play in DJ booths that are removed from the crowd, such as on balconies. (Junior Vasquez had his own purpose-designed DJ booth built at the Sound Factory in New York, complete with its own toilet, fridge and microwave oven, so he didn't have to go anywhere near the crowd for the duration of his famous eight-hour sets.)[2] Others employ their own army of heavies to keep approaching clubbers at bay.

Personally, I've always preferred being in the thick of it. Being only feet away from your crowd allows you to really pick up on their vibes, and gives you a far better instinct for what's going to keep them moving.

But faced with an endless barrage of pretentious smart-arses, you can sometimes understand Mr. Moody DJ's position.

---

2. *He had the right idea!*

Tales from the Flipside

There now follows a list of things you really shouldn't say to any DJ, in any situation...unless you actually *want* to be stabbed in the eye with a lit cigarette.[3]

I swear, all of these have happened to me during my DJing career—many of them several times over. Most include suggested responses.

'Look—no-one's dancing. If you play such-and-such a record, everyone will dance.'

'Oh, I'm sorry, I didn't realise you were an off-duty DJ yourself. Feel free to step inside the booth, help yourself to my headphones and records and show me how it should *really* be done!'

(It's no accident that one came first in the list.)

'Can't you play something with a bit of a beat?

'The last time I checked, the only recorded music without a beat was the drone at the end of 'Sergeant Pepper', or the theme to '2001: A Space Odyssey'. Other than that, each and every other piece of music that you will ever hear has a beat. Bye.'

'Can't you play something a bit faster?'
'Don't know that one. Who's it by?'
'Can you play J-Lo?'
'OK. I'll play it as soon as I can.'
'Next?'
"Not right next, but as soon as I can.'
(Three minutes later)
'Where's my J-Lo?'
'Yeah, I told you, I'll play it as soon as I can.'
(Three minutes later)
'You still haven't played my J-Lo.'
...etc, etc, etc.
'Can you play something by Biggie?'
'OK. I'll play it if I get a chance."

---
3. *Who remembers smoking in clubs? Ah, the good old days.*

(Two hours later)

'Bro, where's my tune? You haven't played my tune!'

(The guy expects you to remember him, individually, and the specific tune he asked for, regardless of the fact you've spoken to 50 other people wanting 50 different tunes in the meantime.)

'Can you play something by Kylie?'

(This is in the midst of an R&B and hip hop night.)

'It's an R&B and hip hop night.'

'Go on, just one.'

'No—it's an R&B and hip hop night. People are here to hear R&B and hip hop. I can't play Kylie.'

'Oh go on, you can sneak one in.'

'Listen to what I'm saying. I'm an R&B and hip hop DJ. I don't even own a Kylie Minogue record.'

'Oh go on, it's my mate's birthday.'

(The dull thud of skin and bone striking wall can frequently be heard at this point.)

'Play 'Time Warp'.

'I'm playing R&B and hip hop tonight.'

'No, you're playing 'Time Warp!'

'No, I think you'll probably find that I'm not.'

'Can you play that one that goes 'dum diddy dum diddy... you know—that one.'

'Who's the artist?'

'I don't know. You must know it. It goes 'dum diddy dum diddy'. You know.'

(Meanwhile, your tune is running out, so you turn round to select another one.)

'Hey hang on. I'll think of it in a minute!'

'Are you going to play something good next?'

'Nah, I thought I'd play something shit.'

'Can't you play something, I don't know... a bit more funky?'

(I actually can't think of a response to this one. It leaves me speechless.)

'Do you have any bhangra or Asian music?'

'No, sorry'

'Racist.'[4]

'What tunes have you got?'

'Lots. What do you want to hear?'

'Well, which ones have you got?'

'Around 250 assorted 12-inch singles across three crates from the last twelve years. Feel free to step into my working space and spend the next three hours sifting through them til you find one you like. Have a look through my wallet at the same time if you want.'

'Can I put my coat behind here?'

'When you came up to the DJ booth, did you see a sign saying 'Free Coat Storage Here?' No. In the same way as you didn't see a sign at the bar saying 'Get Your Chewing Gum Confiscated Here,' or a sign at the security check saying, 'Order Drinks Here'. This is the DJ booth. That's the cloakroom. Bye.'

OK, I'm getting carried away now. And that last response was borrowed slightly from 'Pulp Fiction'. But you get the point.

Sometimes, though, it's what's not said that can drive you to insanity. There are two very distinctive types of looks which are exclusive to girls asking for requests, and which you're unlikely to see in any other walk of life.

The first one occurs when a girl, (because guys never do this,) asks you for a tune, and you politely reply that you don't have it. The girl then feigns a look of mock-horror that looks like it's lifted from a 1950s B-movie.

It's not just that, though. She'll then stand there holding the same expression for the next thirty seconds. What?!

---

4. *"Woke"-ism 15 years ahead of the curve!*

What do you want me to say? I don't have it! Sorry! Goodbye!

The other is worse. You get asked for a tune and politely reply that you don't have it. You're then given a raised-eyebrow look that, without words, seems to be saying, 'well, that's not very good, is it? Not really doing a very good job if you haven't got the tunes people want to hear, are you? Don't think your manager would think much of that if I were to tell him, do you?'

It's also very important never to make direct eye contact with any specific member of the crowd—particularly girls. For some reason, if you accidentally do, that person invariably feels instinctively compelled, after a few seconds of pondering, to come up to you and ask you for a dumb request. Let me make this clear. If a DJ just happens to look in your general direction, ***you DON'T have to then come and ask him for a tune***. You really don't.

As many a song has surmised, everybody wants to be a DJ, so they assume they're qualified to give you advice. It's not rocket science, what we do—but there is *some* skill to it! Most people can't tell the difference between a good DJ and a bad DJ—until they hear a bad one play.

It's not just wannabe DJs, either. Soon, you realise that everybody wants to be an MC, too, as chancers try and grab the mic to 'give a shout out to their mates'. This usually ends up being fifteen minutes of incomprehensible ramblings from a guy who's listened to too many So Solid Crew CDs, and who then throws the mic back down complaining 'this crowd is shit', after he's killed your dance-floor stone-dead.

This type of situation can often get out of hand, and wannabe MCs are prone to getting aggressive if you refuse to hand over the mic—as most DJs would. There was a very ugly incident in Birmingham when Shortee Blitz did just that, and ended up being assaulted by a whole crew, who not only kicked him to the floor, but then dropped his own record cases on him.

In my experience, it's just as likely to happen in some outlying hick town than in a city ghetto spot. And believe me, the hick spots can be much scarier. I once made the mistake of giving out a business card with my home number on in one such place. I was greeted the following morning with an answerphone message from some redneck claiming he was going to kill me, kill my parents and burn my house down, his mate pissing himself laughing in the background.

Do I really deserve to get this from playing records for a living?[5]

So if you ever approach the booth and the DJ looks more than a little reticent, maybe you can understand why.

What narks me the most about dumb approaches—particularly the first one listed above—is the suggestion that you, the DJ, don't really know what you're doing and that they, the punter, know more about what records are going to work well than you.

The arrogance! In what other job do you have to put up with people who think they can do your job better than you, regardless of the fact they've never done it before?

(Actually, forget that. Once, on the Deli counter in Waitrose, there was a guy that was convinced he could slice cheese thinner than me and tried three times to walk behind the counter to do it.)

But it's like me walking into Sharon's office on Monday morning and saying, 'no, you don't type a memo like that. You've got the spacing all wrong! If you put the heading in bold and the signature in italics, it'll create a much better

---

5. *Re-reading this makes me realise that career was even more dangerous than the one I now have!*

impression.' Or striding into Kevin's garage and saying, 'if you tighten the nut on that fuel pump using a number five spanner, you'll really notice the difference, trust me.'

Before both I and the rest of the DJ community get a reputation for being miserable and cantankerous, however, (us?), it's only fair I point out that there have been a handful of occasions where I've been on the receiving end of requests that were just plain hilarious. My two all-time favourites were when I was asked, in all seriousness, to play 'Turn Me On' by 'Stuart Little', (she meant Kevin Lyttle,) and 'Ladies' by The 'Ku Klux Klan'. (Crooklyn Clan.)

Another one that had me in stitches was when a pisshead staggered up to the DJ box five minutes after the night had finished, everyone else had left, and everything had been turned off to say, 'C'mon mate—play something a bit faster!' And he was serious!

Other memorable moments include a girl commenting: 'I don't know what it is or who it's by, but it's been on the radio a lot and you can shag to it.' Incredibly, I guessed correctly that she was referring to Bobby Valentino's 'Slow Down'!

I've only come across the opposite of a DJ not being able to remove a persistent punter from the DJ booth once, and that was when Blu Cantrell performed at the upmarket Bel Air nightclub, part of the Belfry complex near Birmingham.

In most cases where artists are booked for PAs, their own DJ steps into the box to control the music for the two or three songs that they perform. In this case, the guy decided he'd quite like to stay on after the PA and play a few tunes himself...then a few more...then a few more, despite the pleadings of the resident DJ, who really wanted to come back. Eventually, the guy had been on for over an hour, and it took every security man in the house to forcibly remove him from the decks.

I've only been offered money to play a track once—and it was a fairly considerable sum at that.

Having been force-fed the tune 'til I was heartily sick of it, I reached the point in early 2005 where I was happy for any opportunity *not* to have to play 50 Cent's ultra-tedious 'Candy Shop'. I found myself playing a quality soulful/R&B set at The Apartment in Swindon, so I happily left my copy at home

What happened? A rich Asian playboy came up to the booth and waved a wad under my nose, offering to pay me for playing...yep, 50 Cent's 'Candy Shop'. The one night of the year I ddn't have it with me.

Nooooooooooooooooooo!!!!!!!!

Trying to salvage the situation, with the smell of fresh cash in my nostrils, I decided I could at least try and sell him a mix CD, which contained the track. I went over to where he was slumped over a table and prodded him.

He fell over, totally knocked out on champagne and had to be removed by the bouncers.

CHAPTER 6

THE LONG AND WINDING ROAD

'Now, if you call me and I'm not around,
I'm probably putting my grind down,
Doing shows outta town.
I'll be the manager, road manager and call handler,
Booking agent, choreographer and tour planner.'
Masta Ace:'The Grind' (2005)

'Woke up this morning, found a letter that she wrote
She said she's tired that I'm always on the road.
Too hard to swallow being alone.
She needs someone at night that she can hold.'

Anthony Hamilton:' Charlene' (2003)

Interested in the effects of sleep deprivation? Get to know a DJ.[1]

Travel on the average British motorway, and after a while you'll see those electronic signs warning you to take a break; tiredness kills. They're mainly there for lorry drivers, but could just as well have been designed for DJs.

---

1. *I can't say that situation has really improved much for me since quitting full-time DJing!*

Tales from the Flipside

When I first started spinning by night, I was still doing a proper job by day. By 1am—peak time in the average club—my eyes were stinging, my brain was on meltdown, and I was ready to drop.

When I made the switch to full-time DJing, my entire body clock shifted to the point that it was almost a physical impossibility for me to drag my carcass out of bed before 11am, and if I went to bed before three I couldn't sleep. One morning I had to get up at 10 for a job interview, and I felt distinctly hard done by. (My schedule has since drifted back to relative normality, I might add. I got up before eight one day this week!)[2]

Everyone thinks DJs just sleep all day. It's true their idea of breakfast time coincides with most office workers' lunch breaks. But it's not laziness, it's only common sense. You have to get your sleep replenishment sometime. And when you're on the road through the night, tiredness becomes a real issue.

When rave and dance culture took a hold in Italy in the mid 90s, there were a series of late-night road tragedies due to kids falling asleep at the wheel and either leaving the road, or crashing into other cars. The problem was that the best nights were only to be found in a scattering of locations, and these kids were driving vast distances there and back in their desperation to find the hot party.

Murray Beeston, promoter of the Dreamscape raves, died in a car crash two minutes from his home in Northamptonshire in 1996. A well-known promoter of club nights in Leeds was killed along with a group of friends on their way from a gig. The drum 'n' bass DJ Kemistry, one half of Kemistry & Storm and one-time girlfriend of Goldie, died the same way in 1999, when she and Storm were driving from a gig in Winchester. While these

---

2. *These days 8am is a major lie-in.*

might not all have necessarily been down to tiredness, it still highlights the perils of through-the-night driving.

The most infamous example of the damage that driving tired can do came in West Yorkshire in February 2001 when motorist Gary Hart, who'd reportedly been up all night on internet chat rooms, nodded off while driving his Range Rover at around 6am, and let it roll down an embankment on to the East Coast Main Line train track. The 4.45am Newcastle to King's Cross GNER train slammed into it at 125mph as a goods train approached from the opposite direction. He survived; ten of the passengers didn't.

And I know how easy it is to do.

I passed my driving test at 17, and was rewarded with my first car, a white Mini, with which I was well chuffed. My two mates Jonathan and Keith passed their tests at the same time. Keith had another Mini. Jon had a beat-up Maxi which he bought for £40, (he later paid twice the car's value to get it towed off the road when it broke down—unsurprisingly—on the way back from a day trip to the South coast), and we were each so gassed up at having our own motors that we went out every night in a convoy of three; we were far too proud to share the next man's ride. For some reason, one of our favourite pursuits involved driving in the middle of the night into Wychwood Forest on the edge of the Cotswolds, reputed to be haunted and linked with the occult, running into the trees and trying to scare each other to death. Don't ask me why.[3]

The Mini didn't last long. It was a Saturday just before Christmas, and I'd been working since the crack of dawn, then been to a party in Slough, then decided, in my infinite teenage wisdom, to go into Central London to catch some

---

3. *Nothing would get me back there now!*

action. Finally, at around 5am, I headed home after being up almost 24 hours.

I don't remember dozing off. I just remember waking to find the car mounting a grass embankment, then spinning 180 degrees, landing on its roof and continuing along the road, sparks flying everywhere. Bizarrely, I do clearly recall thinking 'I could be in trouble here' as I flew through the air, upside-down. I've always been a logical thinker.

Eventually, the car smashed to a halt on the other embankment. Incredibly, in the dark and upside down, I managed to undo the seat belt and climb out through what used to be the window. Even more incredibly, I escaped with nothing other than a graze on my arm. That and extreme shock, as I stood there looking at the remains of my car spilling petrol on to the dual carriageway. At the time, I took it as fate, or some kind of religiously significant moment. I think the truth is I was just damn lucky.

It was certainly a wake-up call—excuse the pun—and from that point, I've always tried to ensure I've stocked up on enough sleep to see me through a late-night driving session. After an experience like that you become far more alert to potential dangers.

One of my most unsettling overseas situations was during my first mini tour of Germany. The promoter and his entourage had driven myself and Simone, a female MC from Nottingham, from Cologne down to Stuttgart—not exactly local at 290km, or about a four-hour drive. I'd naively assumed that we'd all have hotels laid on, but after the gig, at about 5am, it was announced that Simone and myself had to go straight back to Cologne as we had an in-store appearance to do at an HMV shop at 11. Then the guy they'd given us as our driver, a nutter called Raphael, announced with a vacant grin that he'd already been up for 24 hours and was 'totally knackered.'

Any thoughts of sleep on the return run went straight out of the window. One of us has got to stay awake, I reasoned. And it turned out not to be Raphael. Somewhere around Frankfurt, I watched his eyes disappear into a minute squint, before his entire head suddenly lunged downwards and the car started to swerve violently. I grabbed the wheel, and Raphael was made to pull over at the next available service stop and drink two cups of black coffee, straight. Simone didn't wake once throughout and never knew the difference. As none of us would have done.

I'm frequently put in positions like this, and it's a real risk when you're putting your life in the hands of an allotted driver who you don't really know. On a few occasions in Germany I've had to ask my driver to slow down when things have got a bit scary. No speed limit on the *autobahns* out there—and don't you just know it.

It's for this reason that I've always resisted trying to find myself a driver for my UK gigs. I've just never found anyone that I trust enough to do a responsible job.

It's a real drag having to drive yourself—you can't have a drink and enjoy yourself for one thing—but at least I can ensure I take reasonable precautions to get myself home in one piece.[4]

But with the best will in the world you can get still caught out. Kid Fury, my MC who travelled with me to virtually all my UK gigs from 1998 to 2000, will tell you about a time we were driving back from a night in Liverpool. Somewhere around Birmingham, he was woken by the sound of hip hop, slapping and a cold breeze. It was me belting myself around the face, and blasting the car with icy air and loud music to try and stay alert—all the standard tricks.

---

4. *I still do it now, just with different kinds of gigs.*

I picked up a new one from John Peel's auto-biography *Margrave Of The Marshes*, which was finished after his untimely death by his wife, Sheila. Apparently John[5] used to extend his non-driving arm outwards when he was tired, reasoning that if he nodded off, it would fall and startle him. I'll have to try that one.

Of course, it doesn't help if your passengers are snoring wildly as you, the driver, battle to stay awake through mile after mile of faceless motorway. One time, I had two comatose passengers in the car on a return run from Cambridge, when the entire bottom panel fell off the underside of my car. Even after ten minutes pulled over in a layby trying to reconnect it to the bumper with the aid of jump lead crocodile clips, they snored on oblivious. (Another time, me and Fury took photos of one of his homeboys, totally dead to the world on the back seat and dribbling on to his jacket like a baby on the way to a club. We showed the pictures every time he tried to hit on a girl. He never scored.)

It helps if you can settle your body into a regime, and for the two years I held my fondly-remembered residency at The Forum in Cardiff, I got it off to a tee.

The night was truly groundbreaking. It was one of the biggest and most successful R&B and hip hop nights outside of London, and from 1998, we packed between 1,000 and 1,500 heads into Wales' biggest club every Saturday. A major factor in the event's success was that it was an allnighter running to 6am. The club even cottoned on to serving fried breakfasts around 4.30 to keep the punters in as long as possible. Anyway, for whatever reason, I always drew the final set, so I'd end up staying 'til 6. A hotel every week wasn't practical, so Fury and myself would

---

5. *Another dodgy BBC pervert, it turns out in retrospect. Is nothing sacred?!*

make the 120-mile journey home directly afterwards, (we had an arrangement—he slept, I drove.)

I'd arrive home at about 8am, finally getting to bed at 9. In the Winter, this was no fun. I'd be going to bed in daylight, and by the time I was ready to rise at about 4, it was already dark. That really plays havoc with your body clock![6]

I was amazed to learn that Trevor Nelson, the UK's most prominent R&B DJ, still drives himself to and from his gigs even at this late stage in his career. Trevor admits to being a control freak, and also makes the good point that hours on the road offer the best possible opportunity to catch up on the mountain of new CD listening that DJs have to do, free of other distractions.[7] His six-month driving ban in 2005, however, earned as a result of driving just a little too fast to a particularly hyper track, (Kano's 'Reload'), highlights yet another peril that our breed faces while trying to stick to often hectic schedules!

A hotel is always the most sensible alternative to a long late-night drive. I generally take one if the journey is longer than three hours. (I'm something of an expert on the locations of Travelodges throughout the UK's motorway network.) But there are all kinds of reasons why you might opt not to. Cost is the obvious one, but the benefit of doing a journey in the middle of the night, when you can blaze happily without obstruction, then fall into your own bed at 6am, is most certainly another.

Half the time it's pointless taking hotels anyway. Most UK city centre ones don't have their own parking, so you have to go on a meter. These invariably start charging at 8

---

6. *This sounds horrific to me now and the lack of sunlight in the winter doubtless contributed to the many colds I used to get.*

7. *I do that now with speech-based podcasts.*

in the morning, meaning you either have to feed the meter the night before, or get up early specially. And noisy room maids make sleep beyond 8.30 an impossibility in many establishments.

When it comes to life on the road, schedules and sleeping patterns are something you can control. Something that you can't is the weather. And like lorry drivers, taxi drivers, the police, couriers, and pizza delivery folk, travelling DJs just have to deal with whatever Nature throws their way. There's a job to be done!

It's surprising the degree to which the weather can have an effect on the fortunes of a club night. If you as the DJ take a step outside your front door only to be swept aside by an icy gale, and feel inclined to run straight back into the warm, it's a safe bet any potential clubbers feel the same way. And you're getting paid to be there, they're not!

On one such night, I found myself due to fly to Aberdeen. And if it was that bad down South, I shuddered to think how bad the weather must be up there. Despite Luton Airport being blanketed with snow, the flight took off on time, and all looked good. Until the pilot announced that Aberdeen Airport had been closed in order for snow to be cleared off the runway, and we ended up circling the skies for almost an hour. Just when everyone was convinced we were going to run out of fuel, mercifully, we were allowed to land.

My worst weather experience came almost 11 years to the day after the nodding-off-at-the-wheel incident. On a bitterly cold and forbidding Sunday morning, Fury and myself had just crossed the Severn Bridge and were carefully navigating the M4 near Bristol, when I hit a spot of black ice.

Now, when I visited Tampere, Finland's snow and ice-bound second city, I was alarmed to see cars screeching and seemingly skidding out of control in the main street, until my host explained that all Finns must take an advanced driving test which teaches them how to control a skid by driving into it. Any AA man will tell you the same. But when hurtling towards a central reservation barrier at 50mph in pitch black, take it from me, you don't really have much time to recall the logic. It was roughly the same result as before.

It turned out to be the night that killed poor old Desmond Llewellyn, the guy that played Q in the Bond films. After living to over 80, he died when his chauffered car hit ice and crashed, a really sick twist of fate.

Fortunately, Fury and myself fared better, surviving without a scratch, even though the car didn't. We ended up having to make our long way home via a mismatched combination of trains, buses, taxis, an AA breakdown truck and a snow plough.

Other DJs aren't so fortunate, and the ultimate price was paid by a good friend of mine, Travis, aka DJ Truss in November 2004. Travis hadn't even been DJing the night he passed away. Ever the hard worker, he'd been out distributing flyers in Bristol and was seemingly hurrying to get back to his waiting girlfriend when his car went off the road somewhere in Wiltshire, apparently as as result of hitting black ice.

It was a reminder of how cruel life can be. Travis was one of the nicest, most conscientious and most genuine people you could hope to meet in an industry not well-known for its sincerity. The vast turn-out at his funeral was a testament to what an all-round great guy he was. He won't be forgotten.[8]

---

8. *It's never the ones you wouldn't mind it being, is it?*

CHAPTER 7
DIGGIN' IN THE CRATES

'Put the needle on the record, when the drum beats go like this!'

Criminal Element Orchestra: 'Put The Needle On The Record' (1986)

'There ain't a problem that I can't fix, cos I can do it in the mix.'

In Deep: 'Last Night A DJ Saved My Life' (1983)

*'You can give me some head,
But keep the breakfast in bed.
I'd rather spend my morning digging through some records instead.'*

Dr. Dre Featuring Devin The Dude: 'F*ck You' (1999)

Mark Devlin

The vinyl-versus-CD debate rages on, but the author remains a vinyl junkie and proud of it. Besides, ever tried doing a revolving handstand on a CD?![1]

When meeting the manager of a big commercial nightclub recently to talk about a gig, the guy started showing me the DJ booth. 'You don't use CDs, do you?', he asked, turning up his nose. 'No, mate' I replied, 'I'm totally vinyl'. 'Ah, good,' he said. 'You're a *proper* DJ!'

A comment like that would be dismissed as appallingly Luddite by a whole generation of DJs these days, but it's totally representative of the way outsiders imagine us to perform—with two turntables and a mixer. It's DJing at its most basic, and despite all kinds of new technical alternatives, it's still the method favoured by a vast proportion of the world's DJs.

The question of whether vinyl is finally to be consigned to the history books in favour of digital and electronic formats has been the subject of never-ending debates in recent years.

In my experience, opinion remains more or less equally divided as to the virtues of each. I'm happy to put my hand up in the midst of this and admit to being a Luddite—because I know I'm not alone, and if I start to lose the argument, there are hordes of fellow vinyl fiends that will leap to my defence. But in the interests of fairness, I do recognise there is another side to the argument, and certain aspects of it do make good sense.

---

1. *This one's a real snapshot of a bygone era as both vinyl and CD have now all but disappeared, DJ-land being almost completely ruled by laptops and USB sticks.*

Tales from the Flipside

My DJ friend Ussherman is the sort of guy that calls a spade a spade, and likes to analyse a situation in its most basic form. His recent observation used the same style of logic that views football as 22 men kicking a bag of air around a field and attempting to get it between two bits of wood linked by some string. 'I just don't understand,' he said, 'why in the year 2006, people still think it's a good idea to play music by dragging a piece of stone across a circular slab of plastic.'

Sure enough, many progressive DJs/ producers/ music makers binned their vinyl years ago, dismissing it as a tired, outdated relic of the analogue age. And the fact that as a consumer, you can no longer buy vinyl copies of new album releases in 99 per cent of High Street retailers has to tell you something. Hell, even my Dad listens to CDs now!

The pro/ anti-vinyl arguments come from different sides of the musical fence. It's DJs from the dance music world—house, trance, techno, etc—who tend to favour the new electronic methods, while those on the urban side—hip hop, R&B, reggae and drum and bass—are the root exponents of the 'vinyl lives' movement.

It's not hard to understand why. Hip hop and reggae are close cousins, both having emerged out of the Jamaican sound system culture from an era before electronic methods were on offer, and where the emphasis was on turntable trickery—beat matching, spinbacks, rewinds, etc.

The dance music scene, having evolved much later, and spun off in many different musical directions, is less steeped in the culture and lifestyles of its creators, so has spawned a more experimental and forward-thinking mindset. Naturally, this has gravitated towards whatever new technology becomes available.

And what's available is impressive by any standard. The first challenge to vinyl's monopoly came with the advent of commercial CDs in 1983. Since then, the manufacturers, (with Pioneer and Denon leading the field,) have been one step ahead of whatever objection the vinyl brigade have put their way.

You can't mix on CDs? OK. The early basic models were soon replaced with designs that incorporated the vari-speed pitch controller found on turntables, enabling DJs to speed up or slow down the tempo of a track so it matches the one that's already playing.

It's the tactile nature of vinyl that appeals? The fact that you can actually touch it that brings control? Well, waddya know? The next-generation CD models bore more than a slight physical resemblance to a turntable. The Pioneer CDJ-1000 has become the industry standard, and is now requested in the performance rider of many an international DJ.

The focal point here is a large wheel deliberately designed like a turntable platter, which allows you to cue up, stop, start, scratch and spin CDs back in just the same way you can with vinyl. There are additional features which have found favour with the trainspotter producer types, too, such as being able to electronically loop and repeat sections of a CD and play the selection over and over again, and add various effects and samples.

A more recent move has been the introduction of PC-based music systems, now installed in many clubs. They play tunes off hard disk, and are capable of handling an entire night's music output without a CD or vinyl record in sight.

The whole CD versus vinyl debate has been by far the most popular subject on the chat forum running on my website, and Martin Johansson, a DJ from Stockholm, had something to say about this:

Tales from the Flipside

"My biggest hate is this new PC DJ sh##. What's that about? It's so lazy! It bpm's, beatmatches, and even finds the tracks for you! It takes all the fun out of mixing and looking for the track before the other one finishes. I'm sure these so-called 'DJs' are shooting themselves in the foot. How long before the computer mixes itself and starts making customer announcements?!"[2]

On top of that, there's now an incredible product called Serato Scratch, largely used by American DJs, specifically created out of the observation that many vinyl jocks are loath to give up the DJing format they know and love the best. There are a handful of variations on this, notably Final Scratch, favoured by many UK DJs.

It's a software package which, once loaded into a mixer's memory, allows DJs to manipulate electronically stored tracks by still using a piece of circular plastic—except the sound output has nothing to do with the turntable. The fake 'record' is there as a hands-on tool to allow mixing techniques and trickery to be applied to the electronic track playing.

DJs can be a fairly self-important lot, so it's rare to find a character that virtually all other DJs agree is a master. In hip hop, that accolade belongs to Jazzy Jeff. Sure, the same Jazzy Jeff that partnered Will Smith on 'Summertime' and 'Girls Ain't Nothin' But Trouble', but don't get it twisted! This guy is an absolute beast at rocking the crowd, and the first time I saw him play live he was using Serato. Jeff chopped and ripped frantically through breaks, changing tune on average around every 30-45 seconds, and mesmerising the crowd with his flying hands. A true master at work, and a shining example of what can be achieved with new technology while still retaining old skills and techniques.

---

2. *Not long now, mate, I'm pretty sure!*

It's mind-boggling stuff to someone who grew up in a household where their Dad referred to the record player as 'the gramophone', (and the radio was the 'wireless',) and whose fondest childhood memories involve coming home from Woolworths with the latest chart hit pressed neatly on to a seven-inch slab of plastic, (especially if it was Kim Wilde or Clare Grogan on the picture sleeve!)

And this, I feel, is the main thing that keeps the vinyl market alive—pure nostalgia. Like books, every record tells a story. Glance at a sleeve and you can remember precisely what period in your life you were at; what job you were doing, who you were hanging out with, and who you fancied.[3]

Can a generic CD in a transparent sleeve with the track listing scribbled in permanent marker ink ever compare? I know damn well an electronic icon on a computer screen can't!

Even the faintly musty smell of an ageing record sleeve can send a tingle down your spine... or is that just me?

There are assorted other pro/ con arguments. Here's a summary from Martin in Sweden from another of his forum posts:

'I'm doing my first all CD-gig this week on Numark CDXs, (which is as close to vinyl as you can get. There's actually a real piece of vinyl attached for controlling the sound!)

My feelings before this event. Benefits:

*Not having to worry about skipping needles.

*My back will be aa-iiight the day after—even though I'm bringing ten-times more music than I usually do.

---

3. Though I am now slowly selling off swathes of my vinyl collection, partly to free up space, partly to make some cash, and partly to let go of such physical attachments to this earthly realm.

*Not having to be so selective before the gig. (Three crates is usually the maximum I can physically carry!)

Concerns:

*What do I do if a player breaks down on me? (This is virtually unheard of with Technics turntables.)

*Having to flip through all of these small sleeves and stuff. Recognising 12"s in a crate must be easier.

*Recording my new 12"s into the computer and burning them on CDs isn't really what I consider fun.'

OK, that's added a bit of balance. However, in my unwavering support of vinyl, I have to point out another aspect that just can't be replicated by CDs. The pure theatre of watching a truly skilled DJ performance.

There was a famous statistic that got banded around a few years ago to emphasise the rise in DJ culture. Some time in the mid 90s, global sales of Technics turntables outsold those of electric guitars for the first time. Instead of playing air guitar with a tennis racket, kids had become more interested in 'mixing it up on the ones and twos.' (I caught this fad early. I can clearly remember attempting to scratch-mix some of my Dad's rare Beatles 7-inches on the 'gramophone' at home. Take it from me, kids—turntablism and domestic record players don't mix, and my Dad has the records to prove it.)

The fact that a performance with two slabs of plastic and a mixer can actually offer something visually riveting, as well as audibly, was recognised early on. In Britain, it was the DMC organisation that first saw it, and it's been the world's most enthusiastic exponent ever since.

DMC was started in 1983 by Tony Prince, himself an ex-Radio Luxembourg and mobile DJ.[4] Back then, it was

---

4. *And now yet another deeply suspect character from the world of DJing, having turned up at Jimmy Savile's funeral flashing the "devil's horns" to photographers.*

known as the Disco Mix Club—very much a product of its time—initially as a method for working DJs to get hold of exclusive mixes of current tunes.

But as early as in its first year, DMC also introduced its now legendary DJ Mixing Championships, which still run globally[5] today. Although primarily designed to allow creative DJs to showcase their technical abilities, it didn't take the contestants long to realise that the visual aspect to what they were doing was just as important.

The early tricks involved using body parts to scratch the records and manipulate the mixer's crossfader—elbows, chins, noses, stomachs, then feet, (America's Cash Money was particularly adept at this.)

Trust me, it takes a fair degree of skill to perform a decent scratch with your hand, let alone cocking up your leg and doing it with your shoe!

By 1987, the body parts were already old hat, and the turntablists started coming up with other gimmicks. They got cocky, performing little dances while they were mixing, and taunting fellow contestants by cutting up little insulting messages they'd had specially cut to vinyl—the DJ equivalent of 'ya mama' jokes!

Then things got really crazy. A contestant started scratching with a snooker cue, prompting Record Mirror columnist James Hamilton to write; 'they're scratching with everything but the kitchen sink these days.'

You guessed it. The next year, while UK champ Chad Jackson scratched with a chair, Manchester's Johnny Jay turned up with a bona-fide stainless steel kitchen sink straight out of Do It All, and started mixing a record via a rubber grip fixed to one of the corners!

It was the 1998 German champion, the imaginatively-named DJ David, that left observers

---

5. *(Again!!)*

open-jawed, however. In a fiendishly conceived move, at the tail end of his winning set, he performed a full handstand on one of the turntable platters, and allowed its rotation to spin him round in the air as he balanced. I was there at Wembley Arena when he did it, and you could hear the gasps.

Back on the chat forum, the visual appeal of vinyl performances was raised by DJ D, Australia's number one female turntablist. (Although she's dabbled in Final Scratch, D still prefers spinning off vinyl—and if she can hump heavy-ass crates weighing 40 kilos or more up flights of stairs for a gig, what the hell are the rest of us complaining about?!)

'Hypothetically, if we were to see an increase in future 'CD' DJs, this could work as a plus for us existing vinyl addicts. It will retain a niche, making what we do somewhat 'rare' and 'special'. In this case vinyl could never die.'

Good point. And in an earlier post:

'It seems like the consensus is to go vinyl. This is truly my choice being a turntablist, and when I play this is what I use. None of this jumping back and forth between CD to vinyl, I stick to it, juggle it, scratch it, use body tricks, and love it not only for its rich warm sound, but for its feel and even its show factor. I mean, what's more interesting? Watching someone spin vinyl, or watching someone push buttons?!'

Admittedly, such over-stated theatrics as DJ David's are pretty kitsch by today's standards. In the 2000s, turntablism is no less creative, but is considerably more cool. Now, you get guys like America's Roc Raida or the UK's Scratch Perverts arguing that a turntable is a bona-fide musical instrument; in manipulating it to the full extent of its creative possibilities, it's no different in principle to creating music on a piano or a guitar.[6]

*

Vinyl's exponents point to the basic practicality and flexibility of vinyl. But if the truth is known, there's more than a hint of misty-eyed nostalgia in most of their arguments. Most vinyl DJs are trainspotters, and that's what it all comes down to.

You know you're a trainspotter when you actually take a packed lunch to a record store. I've only done this once...and it was a bag of snacks from a grocery store, so I'm not sure if it still counts...but it was at Rock & Soul Records in New York, arguably Manhattan's finest vinyl emporium. Stepping in there is the DJ equivalent of an alcoholic being locked in a brewery for the afternoon. It's the only form of shopping I can bear.

You might also find yourself admitting to an obsessive disorder if you move into a new house and start putting vinyl in the kitchen cupboards. Yep—I've done this one too, and my wife will confirm it!

I'd moved from a ground-floor flat, where the weight problem of vinyl was never an issue. Arriving at the house, it was clear the upstairs bedroom floor was never going to take it, so ground floor storage was the only option.

Giving into the missus' exasperation at never being able to find a saucepan, I ended up hiring a carpenter to construct a series of made-to-measure wooden shelves for the garage, which got rid of two or three thousand or so. There are still space problems posed by the remaining seven or eight. An obvious answer might be to sell some...but

---

6. *There are also spiritual components to the rhythmic scratching created by turntablism according to the researcher known as Black Dot—see 'Musical Truth Volume 2.'*

that's like asking David Beckham to give up his personal stylist!

Sadly, I didn't count on the effects of a damp Winter out among the spiders, and when I came back to my beloved records the following Spring, I was horrified to find the sleeves all wrinkled and cobwebbed-up. For a while, I speculated on the idea of installing a permanent heater in the garage to keep any further damp at bay, but I conceded that this might be going a little too far!

Wrecked sleeves aren't always a bad thing. There are certain records I play out virtually every weekend of the year where the paper sleeves are so worn they're actually turning into powder. That's good—shows an active DJ! I'm always suspicious of those who manage to keep their tunes in mint condition, all nicely indexed in PVC covers. You need to get out more, son!

I also actually quite like to hear the crackle of vinyl when it's playing. It's just got an air of authenticity about it.

Trust me when I assure you that scenarios such as this will draw nods of recognition from armies of incurable vinyl junkies out there. Like government sleeper agents, there's far more of us than you might think![7]

---

7. *And many, many more of them, it now turns out!*

CHAPTER 8

THE OTHER SIDE OF THE TRACKS

'People, let me tell you,
I work hard every day.
I get up out my bed,
I put on my clothes,
'Cos I got bills to pay.
Now, it ain't easy,
But I don't need no help.
I got a strong will to survive.'

Clivilles & Cole: 'Pride (A Deeper Love)' (1992)

'You want what with me?
I'm a tell you one time, don't fuck with me!
Get down, 'cos I ain't got nothin' to lose.
And I'm having a bad day,
Don't make me take it out on you!'

Ludacris: 'Get Back' (2004)

From master diversion-tacticians, to human road humps, the DJing world is not without its obstacles.

You get little outside sympathy when you moan about the negative aspects of DJing. You're more likely to get 'well, you could always go out and get a proper job', along with a sarcastic smile.

Don't get me wrong. There are both positive and negative aspects to this profession and, as far as I'm concerned, the positives far outweigh the negatives. Otherwise, why would any of us do it? DJing is unlike almost any other job, with the possible exceptions of sports stars, musicians, actors or models. These are the only other jobs I can think of where everyone doing them, without exception, is doing them because they want to. The world will never need to worry about a shortage of DJs.

The problem is, most outsiders think DJs are having a bit of a laugh. That they're overpaid, their life is all wild parties, sex, drugs and getting up late. And they only work at weekends.

Since I've earned a living as a self-employed DJ, it's true that I'm only generally seen out at weekends. But the rest of the week is far from a holiday. When I'm not writing for magazines—my plan B—the entire remaining working week can quite easily be swallowed up doing all the turgid boring stuff that's still an essential part of the job; invoices, contracts, accounting, charts, e-mails. But by far the bulk of the work, if you're not fortunate enough to have a reliable agent to do it for you, comes from actually scoring and setting up the gigs themselves.

Unfortunately, the characters that inhabit the world of clubs tend not to be the most reliable, professional or trustworthy bunch you're ever likely to meet. The average gig will probably take between six and ten phone calls to actually secure, which may take as many weeks. A standard pattern involves about six attempts to pin the promoter down, after which, when you've finally got through, he'll claim he's got another call coming in, and can you call him next Tuesday.[1]

Then you finally secure the booking, and all looks well. Until 6 o' clock on the day of the gig, when the promoter calls to say he's had to pull it because the manager's cat's died, or something equally convincing. Sometimes, you get three of these in a week, and you wonder why you're mad enough to carry on.

Yeah, you take a lot of knocks as a non-superstar DJ.

For some reason, promoters and clubs of the less professional variety, (trust me, they're out there!) seem to think it's OK to pass their misfortune on to the DJ when they have a bad night. You only need to see the guy shuffling nervously towards you and taking you aside to know his next line is going to be, 'listen mate, I've had a really tough night. I can't manage the full amount, so I'm going to have to pay you half instead.'

Where's the justification here?! It's the DJ's responsibility to entertain the crowd. It's the promoter's responsibility to ensure there's a crowd in the first place. If the promoter fucks up on his end of the deal, why should the DJ be made to suffer? Would you say to a plumber who'd come to fix your sink, 'listen mate, thanks for unblocking the

---

1. *The career I've since embarked on, as an author and public speaker, has many parallels to the DJing game, particularly when it comes to setting up speaking gigs. If any event organisers I've worked for over the years feel I've been a little pushy, I apologise, but maybe these accounts will explain how these methods got ingrained in me!*

sink, but I'm only going to be able to pay you half what we agreed. I've just had a really big phone bill'. Would you say to the checkout girl at Tesco, 'sorry darling, I've only got enough for half these groceries. I've had a bad day on the horses.'

And what am I supposed to say to my mortgage company? 'Sorry folks, but I've had a bit of a tough month. You don't mind subbing me 'til next time, do you?'

There's grief to be had from other quarters, too.

There's only one breed of person in the world worse than politicians, tax inspectors, traffic wardens, wheel clampers and speed camera processors.[2]

The doorman on a power trip.

Because standing outside for six hours in the freezing cold looking like The Missing Link is all many of these guys are capable of, (not all, before the doormen of the world start picketing against this book!,) they really do take their frustration out on everyone in sight. They seem to think the criteria on which their role is judged depends on how long they can make people wait in the rain and cold, how long they can maintain a conversation on whether a sports shoe is actually a trainer, and, generally, how much they can behave like the police, customs officials or the Taliban and get away with it.

It doesn't get much better with visiting DJs, either. I've lost count of the number of times I've struggled up to a front door with two lumbering, heavy-ass record crates, only to have a pair of sumo-wrestlers gawp at me open-mouthed as I lump them up the stairs, giving myself a hernia in the process. About the only thing these dudes are useful for is muscle, and they never offer it when you need it!

---

2. *There are a few more, I now realise!*

They're never near the booth when you want them to be, either. In one of my early local gigs, I was getting a lot of grief from some pissed-up fool who kept reaching across the decks and scraping the needle across a record every time he didn't like a tune. I decided to get him thrown out, relishing the thought of seeing him suspended in mid-air as he's frogmarched to the exit. Where was the nearest doorman? Whining up with two girls about 350 feet away at the back of the room!

(On this note, the award for the most off-key, ignorant door staff has to go to a certain venue in Southampton who, in 2003, insisted I stand in a particular corner of a mat whilst speaking to the promoter, otherwise, I was 'creating an obstruction to the thoroughfare.' (I'd like to see them spell it.) This, despite the fact there was nobody else in the entire lobby at the time. A different bouncer then told me to stop sitting on a table in a corridor. When asked why it was a problem, he took a clear ten seconds to think of a response. ('Because I've just told you!')[3]

Even after the gig's finished, you have further patience-challengers to face. Hardly a weekend goes by without some smart-arse spotting me carrying a record case back to my car and shouting out something like, 'hey, Mr. DJ!' 'WHAT?!!' Do you see a traffic warden in the street and say 'hey, Mr, Traffic Warden!'. No. Do I come into your office and say, 'hey, Miss Secretary!' I don't think so.

Any time after 2am, the only people you're going to encounter in town or city centres are pissheads and the police. The pissheads will try and flag you down because they think you're a taxi. (And I've had three occasions in London where people have actually wrenched open my door and attempted to climb in, a strong argument for always driving with your doors locked!) The police will pull

---

3. *Sounds like a warm-up exercise for Covid many years later!*

you over because they can't believe that anyone out driving after 2am who's not a taxi or a fellow police officer, isn't pissed, or on drugs.

There was one period of about a year and a half where I was breathalysed eight times in or around Oxford. The look of disappointment on their faces when that red light fails to go off is priceless!

Then you have the pissheads who think they're invincible, and that it'll be a real laugh to impress their mates by laying down in the middle of the road, or leaping out in front of an approaching car, convinced the driver won't mow them down.

Don't be so sure, my friend. Don't be so sure!

CHAPTER 9

JOCKING ALL OVER THE WORLD, PART 1

*'I'm in New York at the Puerto Rican Day parade,
Then at night I'm in New Orleans drinkin hand grenades,
Outnumbered by the dozens at the Jazzfest in Mardi Gras.
I used to think that it was way too cold
'Til I went to Canada and saw some beautiful hoes
Now I hit the Caribbean every year in Toronto
Then fly to Illinois to get a taste of Chicago.'*

Ludacris: 'Pimping All Over The World' (2004)

*'Yes, I get it poppin', 'specially overseas.
Japanese girls even love my beat.
They say 'Timbaland, we love you,
'We'd love to do things that you do.'
Even in London they say, 'Tim, we love ya,'
And they call me things like 'wicked' and 'the f-ing guv'nor!'*

Timbaland & Magoo: 'All Y'all' (2001)

*'Who's the best?
From New York to Bogota.'*

OC: 'My World' (1997)

If you thrive on unpredictability, a travelling DJ's lifestyle will suit you fine. If not, try something else!

As recently as twenty years ago, all DJs were like Dave the mobile disco man. It was strictly local gigs, and everything was humble and low-key. If you got a booking in the next town, it was an event.

If you were a specialist DJ, there's no way you could support yourself full-time. You had to have a regular job, with the DJing as a sideline. Things like the soul weekenders that used to (and still do) take place at various holiday camps around the British coast, were the highlight of any DJ's year, and were looked forward to for months.

Fast forward to the present day. It's a different world. Dance music, club culture, and the music output they've spawned are now truly global, having led to some unbelievably prolific careers for thousands of people in the game. Not just DJs, but producers, remixers, studio engineers, promoters, managers, booking agents, press and PR officers, radio producers, web designers, publishers. All have built careers and bought homes off the back of the scene.

And it's not just been the domain of the house/ dance music field, either. Happily, hip hop and R&B has gone the same way—albeit to a lesser extent. Without getting too idealistic about it, the music is now a globally understood language, which is all anyone could have ever asked for back in the day.

I've always loved to travel. I take the view that life is actually quite short, and—as far as we know—you only get one crack at it.[1] There's nothing worse than wasted opportunities, and it's a big, diverse, fascinating world out there. So my aim has always been to see as much of it as I can for as long as I'm able.[2] If you can find a career that enables you to do that as part and parcel of the work, you can't go wrong. I was fortunate enough to get many overseas trips out of my magazine job a few years ago, and happily, since taking up DJing full-time, it's continued.

In this job, the travel is a constant buzz, because it's on the international DJing trail that the wild, the crazy and the just plain bizarre tend to happen.

When people say they love to travel, in reality, they probably mean the same as me, in that I actually hate the travelling part of it. For me, one of the biggest ordeals life has to offer is the long-haul economy class flight, only made bearable by the thought of a great destination waiting for you at the other end. My first flight to Japan, at 12 hours-plus, was enough to convince me that I'd never be able to do the 21-hour haul to Australia in one go,[3] so when I first visited, I had to break it up with stopovers.

I don't know why it is, but guaranteed, if I'm booked on a long-ass flight, wherever there's a concentration of precocious screaming brats, that's where I'm sat. If you want to know the exact seat, it's the one next to the 21-stone guy with so much body fat, there's layers of it drooping over the arm into my seat. On the other side is the guy with B.O,

---

1. Or maybe not! But either way, we should still give it our best shot!

2. in 2020—like so many, I suspect—I was convinced the gig was up and I'd never be able to travel internationally again. It made me grateful that I'd seen as much as I could of the world when I had.

3. In 2023 I did!

halitosis and flatulence who chose the curry for dinner, and in front of me is the neurotic woman who can't sit still, and spends the entire 12 hours repositioning her head every twenty seconds.

Other spirit-destroying experiences have included sitting next to an idiot who spent the whole flight trying to chat up the stewardess in his unfeasibly annoying Mancunian whine, (think Noel Gallagher on acid,) and spending seven hours opposite a blocked toilet with a broken door.

Movies are an essential way of passing the many turgid hours—when they can be understood. I was on a return flight from Tokyo when the English-speaking channels had bust, leaving only the Japanese ones to watch. It was 13th September 1996, the day Tupac Shakur died, and I remember seeing news footage showing scenes of some street graffiti, with the phrase 'live by the bullet, die by the bullet' evidently translated into Japanese subtitles.

I've only met one famous person on a plane, I regret to say. It was Sean Penn in LA and, true to character, he wasn't in the mood to chat.[4] Other than that, I once bumped into Pete Tong in an airport queue in Paris, and once saw the actor Tim Roth collecting his baggage at Heathrow. But that's it.

It was on a plane, however, that one of those bizarre moments of synchronicity that everyone seems to experience in their life took place. I was boarding a return flight from Jamaica, when I noticed that already on the plane were the manager of the nightclub I played at in Bristol, Tricky, the artist, and a doorman from The Park End Club in Oxford, all totally by chance. I mean, What are the odds of that?[5]

---

4. *Once an asshole, ...*

5. *The coding of the simulation arranging itself???*

It's when you arrive at your destination that the fun begins, and one of the best things about overseas gigs is when you're met at the airport by the promoter, who then acts as a tour guide to the city where you've just landed.

One of my best experiences of this was when I touched down with my girlfriend Parveen in Tampere, Finland's ice and snow-covered second city, about two weeks before Christmas. The promoter was an African, and I was baffled at how he managed to put up with such a bitterly cold climate. I've got a very high resistance level to cold—I think I have eskimo DNA—but even I was dying from frostbite. He proceeded to give us a potted account of life in Finland. First, how the crime rate is non-existent, and to prove it, he left his car unlocked and still running as we went into a restaurant for an hour. I'd give it no more than five minutes in London.

He also told us how Finns are all technically-competent, to the point that even the OAPs use mobile phones and e-mail daily, but how there's such a trend towards self-sufficiency that there's a very high suicide rate as a result, as people feel unloved and cut off from humanity.[6] Such anecdotes and maxims are priceless in absorbing the flavour and character of a place, and are something you'd never pick up from an official tour.

It's nothing unusual for your contact not to be at the airport as arranged, however. On my 6am touchdown in Larnaca, Cyprus after a night flight, there was no sign of my pick-up, so I had to take a taxi to my hotel in Ayia Napa. The fleet didn't look in the best of shape, and I should have known something wasn't quite right when the door handle snapped off in my hand. Nevertheless, the driver seemed keen to earn my fare, so he chucked the handle on the back seat and off we set.

---

6. *And this was in 2003!*

About two miles into the dusty, barren landscape, an entire piece of the underside of the car sheered off, exposing the surface of the road, and leaving my seat hanging precariously above it. The driver seemed totally unperturbed, and amazingly, we made it.

*

When it comes to arranging overseas trips, the intention is always to space them evenly throughout the year. I usually fail miserably, purely because your control over such matters is limited when you're relying on promoters to book you. You just have to go with whatever dates they offer.

I don't know why it is, but these never end up being distributed neatly. It's more likely the case that you have two solid months at home, at the end of which you're climbing the walls with boredom, then you have three foreign gigs in rapid succession, leading to near exhaustion by the end of it. I've had to get off a plane from Dusseldorf and straight on to another for Los Angeles, straight off a flight from Johannesburg and on to one bound for Vienna, and on one memorable occasion, Prague, London, Amsterdam, Bangkok and Taipei all in the matter of two days.

One of the biggest horror stories you read about in interviews with travelling DJs is airlines losing their records. Some are never seen again, some re-appear after a short while. Whatever the case, DJs value their records with their lives, and most would rather lose a wallet containing their credit cards and their housekeys than lose their records.

It's happened to me twice. Once was an experience with Ryanair. The airline deposited Parveen and myself safely in Dublin, but after an hour waiting aimlessly at the baggage carousel, it was clear my record case hadn't enjoyed the same fortune. The nonchalant response from the airline was to offer to have it flown in at 8am the following morning—not much use when I was due to DJ at 12' o clock that night. After being forced into using the club resident's records—something any DJ hates—we arrived back at Luton the following day to find my record case sitting in the middle of the arrivals hall, and nobody to explain why. But then this is Ryanair.[7]

The other time was at the hands of Air India to New York. Ah, the things we do for cheap flights! It's not that I have any kind of prejudice against Air India. It's just that the check-in process at Heathrow can take nearly as long as the journey itself. The problem is that their London to New York flights generally come in from Delhi first, and are packed with families seemingly relocating from one continent to the other. Mum's there, Dad's there, Auntie, Uncle, Grandad, cousin, etc.. Five suitcases is about the average.

After landing at JFK, I waited at the baggage carousel for my case to appear...and waited...and waited. An hour later, when there was only myself and a cleaning lady in the hall, I realised something was wrong.

On this occasion, I'd put my records inside my suitcase for ease of transportation. For whatever reason, A.I had got me to New York, but had left all my stuff in London. I was told it would be 24 hours before they could get it in on the next flight, so I spent the next day and night with just the clothes I was wearing, having to go out to buy essentials like a toothbrush and deodorant.

Sure enough, the case was delivered to my hotel the next day. Good. Except some idiot had applied the padlock that had been hanging loose off one of the zips. The whole reason I hadn't applied it myself is because I didn't have the key. So I ended up having to cut open the lid with a pair of scissors, and go straight out and buy another suitcase.

---

7. *To be fair, Ryanair have changed since. They've got worse!*

CHAPTER 10
GROUPIE LOVE

'So I get off stage, right?
Drop the mic,
Walk up to these hot chicks and I'm all like
'Sup ladies, my name's Slim Shady,
I'm the lead singer of D12, baby.'
They're all like, 'oh my God, it's him!
Becky, oh my fucking God, it's Eminem.
I swear to fucking God, dude, you fucking rock!
Please mister, please let me suck your cock!'

D12: 'My Band' (2004)

'Girls used to diss me,
Now they write letters 'cos they miss me.'

Notorious B.I.G: 'Juicy' (1994)

'Back then, hoes didn't want me.
'Now I'm hot, hoes all on me.'

Mike Jones: 'Still Tippin' (2005)

"Now, I ain't sayin' she a gold-digger,
But she ain't messin' with no broke niggaz!'

Kanye West: 'Golddigger' (2005)

Mark Devlin

It's always good when fans show how much they appreciate you. But why do they have to wait til you're married?![1]

When I first met the girl who became my wife and I told her I was a DJ, she was distinctly unimpressed, rolling her eyes as if to say 'you're going to have to try harder than that, pal.'

I told her I was also a journalist. I had her attention for the rest of the night.

Different things impress different people, and for every girl gassed up by the fact that a guy's a journalist, (she's since become one,) there's a thousand others who'll be a hell of a lot more impressed by the fact that he's a DJ.

The status of the DJ has grown so much in profile that's it's now on a par with that of a pop star. And pop stars get groupies.

Over the years, I've seen some incredible things. I've seen guys with all the facial attractiveness of an anteater and with the overall physical build of Bernard Manning get all kinds of physical attention from the opposite sex, all down to the fact that they play records for a living, (although this almost certainly says a lot more about the girl than the DJ!) Scientists could doubtless find acres of meaning in the exact anthropological reasons.

Blowjobs behind the booth are popular anecdotes among the more wild-living DJs.[2] (This where pre-prepared mix CDs come in handy. Either that or extended 12-inches...if you'll forgive the Benny Hill-ism.) There

---

1. *The line from Depeche Mode's 'Blasphemous Rumours' comes to mind here! 'I think that God's got a sick sense of humour and when I die I expect to find him laughing.'*

2. *But never me. Life is so cruel.*

are some wild stories about the pioneering 70s New York DJ Francis Grasso, for instance, in Bill Brewster and Frank Broughton's excellent 'Last Night A DJ Saved My Life'. Grasso DJed in The Sanctuary, a notorious gay spot where it was nothing unusual for men to be having sex in the dark corners while the club night was in full flow. On his insistence, women were grudgingly allowed in the club, and inevitably ended up in the DJ booth, often on their knees.

There is, however, one rule. And it can never be broken. These types of situations can only come your way when you *already* have a girlfriend!

It's one of the great injustices of life. It's cruelty and unfairness on the grandest scale. For the many years I was single, try as I did—and I did—do you think I could ever get any action in the club, whether in front of the DJ booth or behind it?

(Well, I won't claim it never happened. There was one very memorable occasion on my birthday in Cardiff, when, for the first, and only time in my life, I had two girls competing for my affections, and all over me as a result. It was more down to an existing rivalry between the two females in question than anything else, but I was prepared to let that slide and just sit back and enjoy the results.)

But the point is, there seems to be some kind of radar signal that you unwittingly send out when you're in a relationship, and which is immediately picked up on by the opposite sex. Because from the minute I started going out with my wife, I got attention on a scale that was just never there when I would actually have been free to do something about it. Why did I only get invited to a post-gig session in a Dublin hotel, where the promoter offered to bring over two lapdancers from his own strip club for a 'private party' when I *already* had a girl? (I'm not the cheating type.)

Prior to this, my success rate could generally be summed up by the type of incident at The Park End Club in Oxford, my first residency, where I struck up a kind of ongoing mutual flirtation with one of the barmaids.

One night, she got ridiculously drunk behind the DJ booth, and made it very difficult for me to concentrate on the last hour of my set. I was convinced my boat had come in when I found myself taking her back to my flat. With a glint in her eye she pulled me into the living room, fell back on to the sofa...and plunged, fully clothed, into a deep, child-like slumber. In the morning, she was hurrying sheepishly into a cab before I could put the kettle on, and I never saw or heard from her again.

Most of the time, though, any attention I get in the club only comes when I'm actually *with* my missus. On one memorable occasion in Reading, a girl sat down next to me and started stroking my knee. I quickly introduced her to my wife, who was sitting on the other side, knowing I'd be in all kinds of trouble otherwise. The effect? The hand moved further North.

This amazes me. Girls try the most blatant tactics when it's totally obvious that a guy's already with someone. What's going through their heads? Are they arrogant enough to assume that they've got the sexual magnetism to make me want to ditch the girl I'm with and elope with them instead? Like Usher.[3]

Or are they just acting out some kind of psychological power game that's been a part of human behaviour since the caveman era? Sexual politics for beginners? I don't know. I can only offer the advice not to try that stuff when my wife is in visual range unless you want your lipstick smeared and your extensions pulled out. (The Reading girl sensed this just in time and made her exit, make-up intact.)

---

3. *Or do his preferences lie elsewhere, as it turns out?!*

Tales from the Flipside

One of the worst examples was one New Year's Eve at a party in Germany, when one particular *schlampe*, as they say in Cologne, was trying every trick in the book to get into my line of vision, and generally piss my girl off. Towards the end of the night, we got someone to take a photo of us as a memento of the event. When I got it developed, I was horrified to see the tart directly behind us in centre-frame, grinning and hoisting up her cleavage. No-one saw her at the time!

Females with issues are scary, and when girls get their talons out, the venom really starts to fly. One such catflight brought a premature end to one of my New Year's Eve sessions several years ago. It spilled off the dancefloor into the ladies' toilets where, for some reason (and don't ask me why,) the mains electrical switch that controlled power to the entire dance area was situated. A few slaps and pushes later, and the entire room was plunged into darkness and silence. It took 45 minutes to repair, by which time everyone had given up and gone home.

There are different categories of *schlampen*, of course. Some are out for the obvious. Others are a little more calculating. Think Janine from '*Eastenders*'. They've heard all the stories about DJ lifestyles, and they assume we're all rich, failing to make any distinction between Spoony and the warm-up guy at the local Roxy who gets £25 quid and a couple of beers per session.

During the time of my residency at The Forum in Cardiff, I travelled there and back every weekend for two years. There was one particular girl that I fancied, (there were hundreds, truth be told, but it's just the one for the purposes of this particular story,) and it must have been pretty obvious that I did.

I asked her out, she agreed, and it involved me driving all the way to Cardiff to take her out to dinner, then home again afterwards, a 240-mile round trip. Plus the Severn Bridge toll. She let me do it twice more, knowing damned well how far I had to come. Only then did she reveal that she already had a boyfriend, and he wouldn't be too happy if word got out I was seeing her.[4]

No such thing as a free lunch? There is if you're a professional goldigger!

---

4. *What is it they say? "Life is for learning"?!*

CHAPTER 11

SHITS, SHYSTERS AND SHAFTINGS

*'I don't want no problems, 'cos I'll put you down
In the ground where you cannot be found.
I'm just Dirt Dog trying to make some money,
So give me my streets and give me my honey.'*

Ol' Dirty Bastard: 'Got Your Money' (1999)

*'The cashier was scared, she asked for my info.
The manager arrived with four guys, that's an insult.'*

Mark Ronson Featuring Ghostface Killah:
'Ooh Wee' (2003)

Dealing in the world of club promoters? It takes a certain strength of character. And a lot of phone credit.

Here's a thought. If there were no dishonesty and mistrust in the world, and it wasn't human nature to lie, there would be no careers for police officers, prison officers, defence lawyers, public prosecutors or half the world's tabloid journalists. That's a lot of people out of work.[1]

It would also mean a hell of a lot of club promoters would be down at the Job Centre, too, because promoters—particularly in the urban music field—tend not to be the most trustworthy breed! They never fail to be entertaining, however, and it's through many years of pursuing them that I've come across the lamest, most shameful and most outrageous lies, excuses and diversion tactics known to man.

(Let me just say at this point, that this in no way applies to all promoters, and it particularly doesn't apply to those that continue to book me. I still have to make a living after this book, and I respect and appreciate all of y'all!)

But as for the rest... A few years ago, I set up a system of logging the daily calls I need to make. I've usually got so much going on, the only way I can keep track of how certain conversations are developing is to keep dated, written notes. A handful of random entries might read: '20/11. X said he'll book me next month. (Course you will, mate. Course you will.)'; '15/12. Finally reached X. Says things aren't going too well for him at the moment. (You don't say.)'; '16/1. X says he'll e-mail contract tonight. (Didn't.); or '18/1. X says he'll call me on Friday. (Lied.)'

The perceptive reader may have noticed a certain amount of sarcasm creeping into the system. It helps me get through the day.

When I can resist the temptation to add my own commentary, however, an ongoing entry might go something like: 'Wed 1/5. X says call him next week;' 'Wed 8/5. X has gone to Miami for a week;' 'Thur 16/5. No reply;' 'Fri 24/5. Says he's had flu. Call him next week;' 'Mon

---

1. *Plenty more than just them, I now realise!*

27/5. Says he's in a meeting. He'll call back;' 'Fri 31/5. Says he's no longer doing the night. Call him next year.'

You get the idea.

It's an exercise in enforced patience, and faced with so much bullshit, the logging system is the only way of keeping on top of all the excuses you're given. But people don't like it when you do. If a club manager says to call him next Friday, I will. In truth, it was probably his way of just getting me off the phone. So when I call next Friday and he tells me he's really busy, and I remind him that he specifically asked me to call on that day, he doesn't like it, and he starts getting defensive.

But then, I guess the way to look at it is, if they're the sort of person that gets upset by you being persistent, then they're not the sort of person you could ever have done good business with.

Soon, you find yourself having to employ tricks yourself just to get people to talk to you. I can make calls without concealing my number, so the recipient can see it's me, only to get the phone ringing forever at the other end, or going to voicemail. I can try again two minutes later, taking care to conceal my number this time, and get an answer straight away. Some people are the opposite; call them from a private number and they deliberately won't answer. You have to let them know it's you before they will. Makes you wonder who they're trying to avoid.

The advent of e-mail a few years ago was a godsend. Now, I can say what I need to say without the expense of many a spirit-zapping phone call. Of course, e-mails can go unanswered. My tactic is to keep re-sending them so many times, occasionally with a prompting prefix like 'are you still alive??!!', that I generally get an answer in the end. Don't get me wrong; I'll happily back off if the answer to a proposition is no. No problem. What I find unacceptable is being ignored altogether. It's just basic courtesy.

You find yourself employing a little amateur psychology before long, trying to predict peoples' mindstates and movements. For instance, don't expect to do business with anyone in the music industry before 10.30am on any given weekday; this industry is not renowned for its early starts. Similarly, very little gets done after Thursday afternoon as weekend wind-down mode sets in. By contrast, I've learned that Monday is the best day to get the most out of music people. Perhaps out of a sense of guilt at having clocked off so early the previous week, people tend to be at their most efficient and productive on a Monday. Just watch those e-mail replies flood in!

From a year-wide point of view, however, you can forget all about the entire month from mid-December to mid-January. Nothing meaningful is going to get achieved this close to Christmas!

Most of the big-shot DJs have managers or agents to handle all this crap for them, of course, but for those not fortunate enough to have that privilege, it can really test the patience.

Through a few years of dealing with this, I've developed many useful tactics and concepts to ease the mental burden. One is the 'one good thing a day' principle. The idea is that, in a sea of negativity, if you can achieve just one positive thing that you can chalk up as an achievement to justify having got up that morning—a booking, a completed contract, a cheque in the post—that's enough. Consider the day worthwhile.

Otherwise, adopt the Fuck It Day principle. A Fuck It Day is when it's apparent that dark forces are conspiring against you in the cosmos, and you're clearly not going to achieve anything worthwhile all day in spite of your best efforts. We all have them. The only option on such a day is to say 'fuck it', and switch on a movie, head to the pub, or do something equally recreational on the grounds that you're not missing any action.

(I was amused to see the Soul Flava promotions crew in South Africa stage a similarly-inspired 'Fuck It Day' as part of their regular weekly programme, meanwhile. This targeted people who were were having a bad week and invited them to say 'fuck it, I need to go out and party and forget my troubles.' A reasonable enough idea. Not sure if it ever worked.)

I was surprised to see the third tactic endorsed by Michael Caine when I read his autobiography 'What's It All About?'. In it, he advocates always having something working for you in your absence whenever you need to go away. If you need someone to make a decision, or mull over something, or you want to outline a project, set the wheels in motion before you depart, then your time away can have some additional value.[2]

I used to take the heavy quota of rejections and general negativity personally, but through conversations with other DJs, journalists, PR agents, record label people, etc, I've come to realise that it's the same for everyone, and it's throughout the music industry.

In clubland, it's often down to the fact that promoting nights proves very attractive to a lot of wannabe entrepreneurs, and they enter into the game not really understanding how hard it is to get it right. Very quickly, they get out of their depth.[3]

---

2. Caine is a Lifetime Actor system asset, of course, but it still stands as good advice.

3. The dynamic's not much different with YouTubers and TikTokers new to the "truth" scene!

There's a maxim that states it's never a good idea to mix business and friendship. And it's true. I played a night in a well-known West End nightspot one December for a female mate, who was attempting to break into the world of promoting, and had become very excited about the 'upmarket', 'exclusive' end of the market—Chinawhite's and all that. She'd entered into a co-promote with a slimy looking git who I sussed straight away as a criminal. She didn't. At the end of the night, he took off with her cash and mine. It was no great surprise to me, but the friendship suffered as a result because I'd tried to warn her.[4]

Some clubs are so dodgy, I'm convinced they're organised crime set-ups, used for laundering money obtained from other activities.[5] On many occasions I've been led through a warren of grim, dimly-lit tunnels to a 'manager's office to find some Jack-The-Lad reclining in a leather chair behind a marble desk, only just stopping short of stroking a white cat, brand new Jag gleaming outside. All that from letting a few punters through the door and selling a few drinks at the bar? I don't think so!

I personally hate promoting, so I do have a certain amount of sympathy concerning the hard work and obstacle-dodging involved. The principle behind DJs staging their own nights is great. The idea is to inject your personal musical vision into an event, and shape, mould and market it just the way you want.

As well as maintaining quality control, there's also the opportunity to make good money. My DJ mate Kieran Hayes started doing this with his own Sweet nights at The

---

4. Can anyone think of anything else many people have been warned against doing in recent years, but they've ignored the advice and gone out and done it anyway?!

5. I wasn't ENTIRELY asleep back in those days then!

Bridge in Oxford a few years ago, which are now among the most respected dance music events in the region.

It's just damned hard work, and you have to be cut out for it. You rarely get a good deal from a club. You want a Friday or a Saturday, they give you every other Tuesday. In the back room. And standing outside clubs at 2am in the rain handing out flyers, and sneaking around city centres pasting up posters isn't my idea of fun.

This aspect of it alone can get you into trouble. There are cartels operating in most towns and cities, whereby one crew controls the market for fly-posting. The correct protocol for any promoter operating on that patch is to approach these characters and pay them a retainer for 'permission' to use these sites. Failure to do so results in your posters being swiftly ripped down at best, or more a hands-on response at worst. The insult is that half the time, the cartels are aren't even based in your town; they can be 50 or 60 miles away!

It's also pretty disheartening when you've spent an hour handing out flyers to eventually walk back to your car and find hundreds of them lining the pavement and the gutter. The times I've attempted to promote nights, I've usually failed dismally, so now I just don't bother.

Everyone should concentrate on what they're good at. Some people are great as promoters. They've got energy, drive, charisma and the ability to charm their way out of a brown paper bag. Me, I discovered long ago that I'm at my best when channelling my energy into either playing music or writing about it, so I leave the promoting to others.

Sometimes, events really are out of a promoter's hands. Darren Goulbourne who stages the Roadblock R&B jams in Hull will tell you that. I'd been hearing good reports about these for a while through my Blues & Soul job, and spent a good couple of years trying to convince Darren he should book me.[6] Finally, he gave in, and I was scheduled to join an all-star DJ cast for a pre-Christmas event at LAs nightclub.

Thirty seconds before midnight, I plugged in my headphones, put on the first record, and lowered the needle. At that precise moment all the lights in the club came on, a deafening alarm sounded, and security started herding everyone out.

It turns out that Lonyo, the star live act, had just gone on to perform in the other room, a spectacular pyrotechnic display timed to go off either side of the stage at that moment. It went off as planned. Except one of them got lodged in a huge overhead ceiling fan, promptly setting fire to the years of dust and dead flies that had accumulated, and proceeding to fan the resulting smoke all through the club. Fire and safety regulations forced the venue to close its doors. Five minutes later, 400 bewildered looking people were wandering the rain-soaked streets of Hull wondering what happened. For me, playing at Roadblock was clearly not meant to be.

Virtually the same thing happened at Creation in Bristol just a couple of years later. Again, the needle was virtually touching my first piece of vinyl when—lights on, music off, and everyone out. This time, the gents toilet had apparently flooded, causing water to leak through the floor and seep into the room where the amps and main electrical set-up for the club were situated. So outlandish things really do happen at clubs. Sometimes.

The rest of the time, it's back to the entertaining excuses, and every week you tend to hear one you haven't heard before. It's actually quite amusing.

A scheduled gig in Luton was cancelled because the roof had allegedly blown off the club in a gale. It really

---

6. *I was very pushy back then. Sorry, Darren!*

wasn't hard to establish this as total crap. An R&B and hip hop night in Leicester was cancelled on the day itself because the club had allegedly been double-booked for a line-dancing class. Convincing. One in Scotland failed to happen because the manager had 'lost the key' to the room where the amps are, so he was unable to switch on the sound system, etc, etc, etc . . .

Often with cancellations, you get the impression that the promoter simply realised he'd fucked up and he just wasn't going to get the numbers through the door, least of all be able to pay his DJs. So in an attempt to save face, he concocted some excuse. Well, better that than allowing the DJs to turn up and not be able to pay them, I guess.

On a couple of occasions, I've made the naïve mistake of booking and paying for flights to overseas gigs myself—one in Holland, one in Ireland—with the sworn promise from the promoter that they'll 'refund me when I get there'. On both occasions, not only did the events not go ahead—surprise, surprise—but the promoters in question have been neither seen nor heard of again, either by me or anyone else I've asked. Maybe they put posters up in the wrong spot?

There have been two occasions where I've forcibly frog-marched promoters to cashpoint machines, clearly the only way I was going to get paid on the nights in question. The first one was easy enough. The promoter was of the 'door whore' breed, basically a bimbo that had delusions of being an important promoter based on the fact that she has a clipboard in her hand, but with no clue about finance, hence the walk to the hole in the wall.

The other was a bit more risky. It was in one of Liverpool's grimier quarters, and the promoter had three mates with him. It could have turned ugly, but I was so unwilling to go home empty-handed that the long walk up the High Street was instigated nevertheless. The fact that I was still able to walk back again, let alone have the money in my pocket, was a significant bonus, but a risk that had to be taken. You can only take so much.

DJ solidarity can be a powerful thing. One New Year's Eve not too long ago, I'd been recruited by a Turkish promoter to play at a glitzy venue in Dusseldorf, full of VIPs. Upon arrival, it was clear the joint was an operational establishment for the city's Turkish Mafia. Fortunately, I wasn't alone. A house DJ from Berlin[7] had been hired to play alongside me through the night.

When the promoter started showing increasing signs of shiftiness, we had a quick conference and decided to insist on full payment upfront before we played a single tune. As the only DJs in the building, we kind of had them over a barrel; you can't be without a DJ on the most important party night of the year. We also reasoned that two guys are harder to beat up than one. Our gambit paid off, and the promoter grudgingly handed over the Euros there and then.

It's on occasions where they owe you money when people tend to be at their most entertaining. I'd spent two weeks chasing one such 'promoter' from up North, and the guy had successfully dodged all my calls. One day I caught him off-guard and he answered. When he realised it was me, he switched instantly from his distinctive Yorkshire twang to a laughable attempt at a Chinese accent, blurting out, 'no, he not here right now!' before cutting off the call.

But the most sickening trick of all—and this will shock you—is when people try to convince you they've had a bereavement in the family, purely as an excuse for not facing up to their responsibilities and to buy themselves some time.

---

7. *I can now reveal that this was Marcus Engel.*

I'd never have imagined anyone would stoop so low had I not discovered, quite by chance, that a story given to me by an overseas promoter about his sister dying turned out to be total fabrication; he never even had a sister. I know this type of scenario to have happened at least once more since then. Personally, I'd never want to tempt fate by such deception. Must be bad for the karma.

CHAPTER 12

JOCKING ALL OVER THE WORLD, PART 2

From a Bangkok whorehouse to a Cape Town crack spot.

*'From New York to Cali,
Coast to coast I be rockin' coliseums and clubs.'*

Rakim: 'From New York To Cali' (1996)

*'Now, I'm the type that's always catching a flight.
And sometimes I got to be out at the height of the night.'*

The Roots: 'You Got Me' (1996)

*'London, England, South of France,
And all points between, they know about your man.
Konichawa ladies, when I'm out in Japan.'*

Jay-Z: 'All Around The World' (2000)

Tales from the Flipside

From a Bangkok whorehouse to a Cape Town crack spot.

The more you travel, the more you get to understand that different countries have very different customs and ways of behaviour, and it manifests itself as fascinatingly in crowds' attitudes to DJ performances as anything else.

Whereas in Paris, much as in London, you can expect a generally tepid response from a crowd who are more interested in looking cool at the bar than breaking a sweat on the dancefloor, in Germany, the energy levels are off the meter.

And in contrast with Australia, where a DJ is almost invisible, and too much mic work tends to impede peoples' enjoyment of the music, in many other countries, a DJ is considered as much of a performer as a singer or rapper.

I found this when I first played both Botswana and Mozambique. There, instead of dancing, clubbers will crowd around the DJ booth in a semi-circle avidly watching a DJ's every move, like they're expecting you to do something amazing. Umm, I'd rather you just dance!

The resulting awe and respect that you draw there is incredible. On my first two occasions I was made to feel like a demi-God, people scrambling to touch my hand. It's not something that tends to happen to me much, so I happily absorbed every minute![1]

It's easy to forget how good we Brits have it when travelling overseas. The fact that several million people speak the same language as a matter of course, and virtually all others speak enough to allow you to be understood, is a very real privilege. Even the cab drivers that are sent to

---

1. *I now regularly receive a lesser version of this kind of reverence at the conference events I speak at, and I find it very unnerving!*

meet you at the average overseas airport can hold a decent conversation. Just picture the reverse in London:

Torsten: Guten tag. Sprechen Sie Deutsch?

Cabbie: D'you what, pal? Can't understand a bleedin' word you're saying. Doncha speak English?

Torsten: Bitte?

Cabbie: Look, do you want a ride or not? I ain't got all bleedin' day!'

It pays to get an insight into local customs when visiting a country for the first time. Fortunately, the promotions manager at The Planetarium in Dubai had the foresight to fill me in on their public venue licencing laws before I started playing. I was told that if anyone other than he or I were found inside the DJ booth, he could be arrested and lose his licence. Furthermore, I had to refrain from playing any record containing explicit or obscene language, or the same thing could happen. No 'My Neck, My Back' 'Put It In Your Mouth' or 'It Ain't No Fun (If The Homies Can't Have None)' that night.

I've been both the coldest and the hottest in my life on overseas jaunts. The hottest was Dubai in August. I only left the comfort of my air-conditioned hotel twice—once to head to the club, when the outside temperature was almost 100 degrees even at 3am, the other to take a tourist boat trip along the creek. It was so hot I had to try hard not to pass out.

The coldest was colder still than Finland. It was Oslo in December, where I set off from my hotel to have a look around town, wondering how the streets could be so deserted in a major capital city. Ten minutes later, my hands blue from hypothermia and my brain frozen in my head, I knew. Nobody but me was stupid enough to go out.

Tales from the Flipside

Some newly-visited cities are fairly run-of-the-mill; with the exception of Munich, Hamburg and Berlin, every German city I've been to looks the same.

Others leave a lasting impression instantly. One of these was Bangkok, where I immediately formed a few observations, as follows: the place is a total den of vice, with shocking poverty; it stinks to high heaven of everything from rancid drains to bizarre food smells; there are rats the size of cats; Thai hookers really do holler at you 'me love you long time!'; Thai people are very short (at 5'10", I was a giant); very few white tourists seem to venture out after dark.

Despite the universality of English, hardly anyone speaks it in Thailand. I attempted to tell the first taxi driver I came across to take me to a bar I'd heard was cool, and I was chuffed when he seemed to understand my combination of bad Thai, sign language and pointing at a map.

He took my money, dropped me outside a whorehouse and sped off. After that, I decided it was best to walk.

Which is something you wouldn't want to do in the wrong part of Johannesburg. I've been going to South Africa for the past six years, and have struck up quite a following there now, largely as the result of having regular mixes broadcast on Metro FM, the 24-hour national urban music station which is an equivalent to the UK's Radio One.

SA is smart and presentable. The road system equals anything Western Europe has to offer, and the leisure/entertainment facilities in the big cities just can't be bettered. On top of that, the friendly and upbeat demeanour of black South Africans, who are among the brightest and most colourful people I've met, is definitely uplifting.

It's real country of extremes, however. Although now one of the most prosperous African nations, there's still appalling poverty—particularly evident on the route from Cape Town airport into the city, which is lined with mile after mile of shanty towns. And the first thing overseas tourists hear about when it comes to Johannesburg is its infamous tag as 'murder capital of the world.'

Although this tends to be over-dramatised, it's still an unsettled and hectic city—a shame, as it's also quite beautiful. The average suburban house has at least three permanently-locked security gates and acres of barbed wire as standard, and even the locals won't stop at a red light after dark for fear of being carjacked.

One of the main ghetto spots in Jo'burg is the Yeoville district, not dissimilar in feel to the French Quarter in New Orleans. Although it's the sort of place you really wouldn't want to be walking without the guidance of a local, particularly after-dark, it turned out to be the location of one of my most memorable, and strangely fulfilling gigs in SA.

One of the main nightspots was a joint called Tandoor, famous for its reggae nights. On Wednesdays, these always used to be handled by Admiral, a white guy from London who relocated to SA to make a living as a reggae DJ/ producer, and has done very well for himself as a result, and Appleseed, a Jamaican DJ/ MC.

The place gets rammed, and in the Summer months they open up the rooftop terrace and have cook-outs, making the whole place feel like a miniaturised Notting Hill Carnival. On one of my early visits, I got the opportunity to spin alongside Admiral. I was a little nervous, as this was clearly the sort of raw crowd that would jeer and bay for a selector's blood if he didn't drop the right tunes. Also (and for neither the first nor the last time in my career,) I was one of only two white people in the building.

Tales from the Flipside

Stepping up to play, I was dumbfounded to discover there was only one, battered neglected turntable. Admiral played purely off CD, and I had only vinyl. It's all about adaptability, however, and through a combination of swift handwork, microphone distractions, and much blurred juggling, I pulled it off, and won the respect of the crowd.

I've played all kinds of spots, and this was one of the most unglamorous—a kind of dimly-lit concrete bunker with weed smoke filling the air. It's the kind of spot where your records actually sweat, and where you find DJs plugging their headphones into the microphone socket and shouting into them in the absense of a real mic—a standard 'hood trick. (The other one, just out of interest, is when the output from a turntable is only happening on one of the stereo channels. The cure is to unscrew the head shell, gently lick the metal points on the end and re-screw it. I've no idea what it does, but it cures it every time!)

But it was one of the most enjoyable, because this is the sort of spot where no-one's there to pose and try and look cool. They're there strictly for the music, and the sort of rapport that a DJ can build up in such circumstances is phenomenal. It's almost spiritual.

Cape Town's not quite as intense as Jo'burg, but it still has its no-go areas. Parveen and I discovered this when we went brazenly out from our hotel for a walk one evening. The route took us past a shabby looking café, where a bunch of unsavoury looking characters were huddled round an outside table, flanked by a couple of dudes propping up the street corner, peering at us menacingly from under the brims of their hats. We later found out this was a notorious crack spot, and nobody in their right minds goes near there after dark. Oops.

Other than that, Cape Town is beautiful, and it's not hard to understand why it's consistently cited as one of the world's top five holiday destinations among travel writers. The beaches are great, but swimming is not to be advised. No, not sharks. It's the point where the Atlantic and Pacific oceans meet, and the resulting currents make for icy cold water that bites right to the bone. The locals know this; we didn't. It took us twenty seconds to run waist-high into the water, and two seconds to run out again.

Security concerns can be quite an issue at gigs. In some spots, it's virtually non-existent. The combination of alcohol, late nights, and hundreds of people rammed into one spot are an obvious recipe for trouble.

I've seen many fights break out on the dancefloor with no evidence of security staff around—too busy chatting up girls on the door or whining up in a quiet corner—in which case, you often feel a responsibility to try and put a stop to it yourself. The most effective way is to just cut the music dead—with a mic. announcement asking the idiots to chill, if you're feeling brave enough. Then the entire club looks around to see what's happening, and the antagonists get so embarrassed at being the centre of attention they often just stop and walk gingerly away. It works very well.

I've been lucky in avoiding drama at clubs. I was at Matrix in Reading only an hour before some fool famously managed to get a gun past the metal detectors, and ended up putting a bullet into a doorman, and another into the head of an innocent bystander. Worrying about whether you're going to get shot should never be an issue when heading for a night out. Around 2000/ 2001 in the UK, it became a real problem. Another time, the manager of a club in Cardiff was beaten unconscious when a bunch of thugs jumped the door just a short while after I'd left.

In terms of unusual locations, I once DJed out of the boot of a sports car. It was at the Summer Vibes weekender at the Pontins holiday camp in Camber Sands, as part of some sponsorship deal laid on by Vestax, the DJ equipment maker. I've also played at the massive Mercedes Forum in Stuttgart, where the brand's main car showroom was converted into a club for the night, and in a warehouse next door to the factory where they brew Stella Artois in Leuven, Belgium.

Other memorable DJ booth locations have included one behind the bar at The Aquarium in London—which was certainly handy, one in Switzerland with its own purpose-built toilet—which was very handy, and one in Austria flanked either side by fully-performing pole dancers. Which was very distracting.

Any opportunity to play outside in the daytime offers a much-welcomed alternative to being shut indoors. Unfortunately, such occasions have been quite rare for me, but one of the best was St. Paul's Carnival in Bristol, where I played hip hop to a hyped-up crowd from the back of a lorry parked outside a pub. The weather was perfect. The one occasion I played at Notting Hill Carnival it wasn't; it bucketed down.

The only event I've ever played at that rivals Notting Hill in terms of sheer scale is the Queensday celebration in Amsterdam. This happens every 29th April, when the Dutch nation hits the streets to party day and night to mark the occasion of the Queen of Holland's birthday.[2]

I was there in 1999, and I've never seen so many people crammed into one place. The official figure stood at around three million for the centre of Amsterdam. This one was another blazing hot day, and naturally, opportunities for open-air parties were everywhere. Sound systems lined every street, playing everything from roots reggae

---

2. *Little did I realise at the time, but this was a massive occult ritual timed to mark the important pagan festival of Beltane with orange, a colour associated with Freemasonry, everywhere.*

to hardcore techno. Every time you turned a corner, one bassline would merge into another. The other great thing about such gatherings is the smells, with every type of food under the sun cooking on open grills. These types of events are my favourite in the world, and I wish I could do more.

My first (and only) set at the legendary Southport Dance Weekender could technically be described as a daytime set, too. As is customary with DJs new to the bill, I was stuck on from 6-7am on a Saturday morning, with the sun high in the sky as I finished. Despite the time, there were still around 30 hardcore clubbers left in the room. One of them turned out to be my future wife, but I didn't meet her until over a year later. We also worked out that she'd once been to one of my gigs at Corks in London, but again, it was months before we finally met.

When I later recounted the story to my folks, they revealed that they'd both attended the same dance a year or so before they finally met, and only realised it years later, too. It seems it really is a small, and very strange world![3]

---

3. *I got that right!*

CHAPTER 13

DIALHOPPING

*In the daytime, radio's scared of me,
'Cos I'm mad, 'cos I'm an enemy.
They can't come on and play me in prime time,
'Cos I know the time, 'cos I'm getting' mine.
I get on the mix late in the night.'*

Public Enemy: 'Don't Believe The Hype' (Def Jam, 1988)

*'Good morning and evening friends.
This is your friendly announcer Mr. DJ,
And you are on the wire.'*

The Concept: 'Mr. DJ' (1986)

*'And everything I had to know,
I heard it on my radio.'*

Queen: 'Radio Gaga' (1984)

Radio was made for the art of DJing. What happened?

I actually got into DJing the 'wrong' way round. While most DJs earn their stripes in clubs, then, if they're lucky, graduate on to radio, I did the radio thing first. In a way, this was part of the copping out and taking-the-easy-option that I did a lot of when I was younger.

I'd decided I wanted to get into journalism, and without too much effort, I was accepted by Fox FM,[1] the commercial radio station for Oxford, to help out part-time in the news room. The music/ entertainment/ media industries are fairly unique, in that they manage to get a hell of a lot of work out of people without actually paying them anything in return. The general stance is, 'well, it's a popular game, pal, and it's good experience. If you don't want to do it, there's a hundred other fresh-faced young hopefuls out there who will!' Clubs use this, radio stations use it, newspapers and magazines use it—and it works for all of 'em!

My duties involved things like collating travel news, archiving old stories, making tea (obviously), and the classic ring-rounds of police, fire and ambulance stations that are a daily routine for any newsroom.

I was allowed to work on my own stories, usually nothing more exciting than a weekend jam festival in a local village, or a pigeon fanciers' convention, or on one memorable occasion, a petrol and diesel delivery being mixed up in a fuel station, creating expensive and entertaining havoc. But one time, I just happened to be the only one around when a coach full of American students overturned on the M40, killing one, and I had to go out and do the interviews. It was a sobering introduction to the world of real news.

Anyway, useful as all this was in getting me into journalism, there were far too many other temptations within the environment of a radio station, and before long, I started orienting more and more towards the programming

---

1. *"Fox" equates to 666 in Gematria!*

side. I really picked up on the whole concept of radio. The way it can reach into peoples' lives and connect with them whatever they're doing—driving, washing up, having a bath—really appealed to me. I consider the new phenomenon of internet radio to be severely restricting in such a context, in that you have to be near a PC to indulge—not always convenient!

I thought it was a great way to influence people meaningfully with music, and I wanted in.

So before long, I'd started doing 'tech-op' shifts.[2] This involved the playing-out of pre-recorded shows, bringing in the ads and news at the allotted times, that sort of thing. It was a great way to get confidence in being on air. Strangely, it never fazed me knowing thousands of people were listening to my handiwork, and if I fucked up, they'd all witness it. Why? Purely because I couldn't see them. What did terrify me was the thought of playing live in front of hundreds of people,[3] where if you mess up, you're going to get all kinds of heckles and jeers and glares. This held me back from really applying myself on the club scene for years. I felt safer hiding behind radio.

(The cock-ups did happen, though. Back in 1990, Fox took a syndicated programme called 'The American Top 40' with Shadoe Stevens. For some reason, this was provided weekly in the form of four vinyl records. On one memorable occasion, the needle stuck in the middle of one of Shadoe's vocal links. I panicked and went to move it on, sending the stylus flying across the vinyl. Any listener preconceptions about the show being live were neatly dealt with that day.)

---

2. *Still in the time of analogue reels of tape—another relic of a bygone era!*

3. *Thankfully I later overcame this one.*

I ended up staying at Fox for six years, and at times, it was like my second home. I spent many nights crashed out on the office floor with some snacks from the petrol station for breakfast.

These days, entire radio station outputs are run off computer, but in the early 90s, it was still the era of quarter-inch reel-to-reel tape, and I became an expert in editing with the stuff. I learned how to put together primitive running mixes using three of these machines; they had a vari-speed pitch control, just like on turntables, and this is how I learned to beat-mix. I also established an annual institution. Every New Year's Eve from 1990 to '94, I programmed a live eight-hour music mix that formed the soundtrack for thousands of listeners who didn't want to hire a DJ for their party.

For my last three years there, I produced a Friday night show that was broadcast live from a club in Oxford, with Kiss FM's Graham Gold hosting the first year. At the time, this was still a pretty revolutionary idea.

The music side of radio is notoriously difficult to get into. So you tend to stay put and guard your position jealously until something better comes along. In 1996, something did, and this really was the turning point in my success as a DJ. Galaxy Radio in Bristol, then still a meaningful and highly respected specialist station, liked my demo, and hired me to present a new Friday night R&B and hip hop sequence called 'The Swing Shift.'

It was a great position to have. The station reached around three million adults in the South West and Wales, mine was the only specialist show dealing with my type of music, and I got to select all the records myself with no outside interference. It was something any other DJ playing my music would have killed for.

Tales from the Flipside

I soon realised what a privileged position I was in. Back in '96, Westwood and Trevor Nelson were still the obvious big names on Radio One. Then you had Matt White and Shortee Blitz on Kiss. Beyond them, there were just half a dozen out-of-London jocks who got invited to record company shindigs and to interview overseas artists when they were in town.

You had Simon 'Schoolboy' Philips, KC and One Step on Galaxy Birmingham, Erroll Phipps on Galaxy Manchester, DJ Fluid on Galaxy Leeds, DJ Diggz on Galaxy Bristol, and me. For a couple of years, we were deemed the most influential urban music radio DJs in the country, and all the record companies treated us like gods. (It was illuminating to note how quickly the 'how's it all going?' calls from the record companies dried up the minute I stopped doing the show!)

But you're never going to take up a position like this without getting somebody's back up, and in Bristol, there was a lot of it. The city has a reputation for being hostile to outsiders, and the fact that I was from Oxford didn't go down too well in certain quarters. I went to great lengths to try and ensure things were kept amicable between myself and the parties concerned.[4] I invited just about every other urban music DJ in the region to come in and do guest mixes on my show, to keep up good relations. Of course, none refused. But the bitching continued. Let's be real, would any of them had done any different if they were given an opportunity like mine? Of course not. They'd snap it up in a flash, just like I did.

*

---
4. *Oh, how I'd do things differently if I had my time again!*

Radio DJing requires an entirely different approach to playing in clubs. Any DJ worth their salt won't pre-plan a club set; it's all about instinct and spontaneity. On radio, everything has to be pre-planned. There are formats and timings to be stuck to, and there's a lot to do on a live show. If you haven't planned it down to the finest detail, it'll show, and it'll end up a chaotic mess.

Most people who've never visited a radio studio imagine the set-up to be like TV; a dedicated team working away like cogs in a machine, each performing their own vital role. The truth is, more often than not, it's just the presenter alone in a studio, often in the entire

building. You alone are responsible for the station's output, for playing the ads, answering the phones, letting guests in through the security door, everything. Sometimes it gets hectic.

On top of that, all stations have what they call an 'obit alarm'. This is triggered remotely in the event of a member of the Royal Family dying, and emergency broadcast procedures are put into place. Every radio DJ in the world prays they're not the one on-air when this happens. In my Galaxy days, everyone assumed it would be the Queen Mum next to go. When it was Diana, it knocked the entire station for six.

I'd been kipping down in the Galaxy offices after a club gig the night it happened. I awoke around 6am to find the building buzzing, journalists flitting about, TVs blasting. I asked one of the journos what was happening. His words 'Princess Diana's been killed in a car crash' took some sinking in. It was this generation's own JFK

moment. (The other one was 9/11. I heard the news while holidaying in Tongue, in remotest North-West

Scotland—a setting as far removed from the carnage in Manhattan as it's possible to get.)[5]

I soon discovered one of the biggest challenges to playing hip hop on the radio was keeping the output clean. Although you can hear the most hardcore swear words on TV after 9pm, on radio, even the lightest of expletives is disallowed.

My tape-editing skills came into play here. Any curse-laden track I wanted to play would go straight on to a reel, then the offending word would be sliced out and quite literally reversed, so fuck became 'cuff', shit 'ish', and so on. After a while it becomes like a language, and when you hear a track saying 'cuff all y'all muthanickuf saa-chib ziggin', you know exactly what's going on.

The most work I ever had to do was on 2Pac's 'Hit 'Em Up', arguably the track that triggered his assassination; it took 48 razor blade edits before it could be played. You get caught out, though. Lil' Kim's record company mixed up the labels on one of her tracks once, so the 'clean' version actually sounded like a weekend with the Osbornes. Another time, I let the dirty version of Sporty Thievz 'No Pigeonz' go out and only realised my mistake when the managing director called on the batphone and barked 'verse two, line one, 'bitch'. Verse two, line three, 'ho'. Verse three, 'go fuck your babysitter.' I don't want to hear it, Mark. I don't want to hear it', before replacing the receiver.

Fox's erstwhile managing director, Tom Hunter, was less tactful when he heard Graham Gold playing an offending track on the live-from-a-club programme I was tech-opping. He turned up unexpectedly in reception

---

5. *And actually, to my shame, bought the official narrative back then, so steeped was my consciousness in mind control. Though I did always consider there was something a bit fishy about the "unlucky" death of Diana.*

at 10pm, purple with rage and screaming through the intercom at me: 'tell that c**t if he doesn't get that record off immediately, he's fired!' The irony of his choice of vocabulary was not lost on me.

In Europe, there are no such restrictions. I once sat in on a radio show in Amsterdam, where the DJ accidentally put on a clean version, then, realising his mistake, took it off, live on air, and replaced it with the raw version. And in Germany, everyone thinks you're a prude if you play a radio mix in a club.

It didn't take long for me to become a local household name off the back of the Galaxy show. The club offers came, notably in Bristol and Cardiff, and it was a new experience walking into a club and getting stares from all quarters, and comments like '*that's* what he looks like', 'I thought he'd be older', or 'I thought he was black!'

It also brought recognition of a different kind. For some reason, I became popular with the local prison community, to the point that I started receiving letters weekly, telling me my show was the only thing preventing some of them from doing something crazy. The majority came from Katrina, aka 'Pebbles', on lock-down in HMP Eastwood Park, who became so attached to me she promised to 'look me up and hunt me down' when she got out. Fortunately, she got moved to Eccleshall in Staffs, and I escaped. Never did find out what she was in for. I'd rather not know.

But the best aspect of my Galaxy years by far was the opportunity to meet and interview the artists whose music I played. I got to talk to, among others, The Fugees, Faith Evans, Beenie Man, Kelis, Blackstreet, K-ci & Jo Jo, Warren G, The Beatnuts, Da Brat, Queen Pen, (now a strong contender for 'After They Were Famous'!), Das EFX, Common, Cam'ron, Mica Paris, Angie Stone, Shola

Ama, Kele Le Roc, Beverley Knight[6] and the late Aaliyah, who really was every bit the lovely person the tributes say she was. Finding myself writing her obituary for Muzik Magazine five years later was a bit of a choker.

The liveliest interviewees were Busta Rhymes and Rampage, just as hyper as they sound on track. Missy was stoned in a London hotel suite when I met her, Kelis was shaving her legs, mid-interview, on her hotel bed, Beyonce still had black hair.[7]

Canibus was hard work; he chided me for not listening properly to his new album when I started asking him questions about it. Big Daddy Kane, interviewed in the back of a space cruiser, didn't seem to know what country he was in, Brownstone spent their whole interview time trying to seduce me backstage at the Royal Albert Hall. Which was nice.[8]

UK rapper Ty turned the tables on me and started interviewing me on my own show, commending me afterwards for 'some good answers.'

I went to great lengths, roving reporter style, to get some interviews. I waited outside the Hot 97 building on New York's Broadway for Kool DJ Red Alert to emerge after his radio show, because the army of assistants protecting him wouldn't let me through the door, and ended up talking to him in the back of his limo. I spoke to Funkmaster Flex at 4am in New York's notorious Tunnel, while club staff swept up and threw away bottles around us.

---

6. All with zero idea back then of the extent to which many of them were so utterly owned and controlled.

7. Sitting on a couch next to Beyonce is something that would NEVER happen now. Thank God!

8. Maxee from Brownstone later died in extremely suspicious circumstances. Neither the first nor the last.

I didn't have to try so hard with Guru. I just happened to walk into the Fat Beats record store in Amsterdam, and there he was looking at tunes. He happily agreed to an interview there and then. That's the kind of cool guy he is.[9]

*

Within a few weeks of starting the Galaxy show, it became apparent that people hang on your every word when you're on the radio. You can mention you're planning to hit a record store the following day. A week later you'll meet someone and they'll ask you how the record store trip went, when you yourself had forgotten all about it as soon as you'd left.

But the most flattering and fulfilling variation on this is when someone tells you they went out and bought a record as a direct result of hearing you play it on the radio. That just defines a DJ's true role in one go. Throughout my formative years, there were scores of records that I considered 'Pete Tong records' or 'Robbie Vincent records', or whoever I first heard play them. To attain that influential status as a DJ yourself is just the ultimate.

You can't beat a live radio show over a pre-record, and I'm convinced listeners can tell the difference. Live shows just have a certain edge and energy about them, and I sought to make mine as lively and diverse as possible within this context. When you've got a crew of MCs freestyling live on air, maybe Out Of Da Ville from Nottingham, Born In The Ghetto from Bristol, Ty and Shortee Blitz, Blak Twang, Funky DL, Lethal & Destruction—and no-one in the room knows what's going to be said next—to me, that's the ultimate in taking radio to its limits.

---

9. *Was. Guru is yet another to have passed away in very suspect circumstances, (see 'Musical Truth Volume 2.')*

Tales from the Flipside

It upsets me that so many stations now are just mass-manufactured clones, parts of big, cold, faceless corporations which, like so many other commodities, just treat their stations as money-making entities. Tragically, you're hard-pressed to find any UK commercial stations now that fall outside of this scenario.

Many people are shocked to discover that the entire music output on certain stations is determined by a computer, and 'DJs' are simply there to play what they're told at the touch of a button. In some cases, they're told exactly what to say as well, leaving them as nothing more than human computers. What a waste of such a great medium with so much potential.

And sadly, this was to become the fate of Galaxy. After two and a half great years, a new management regime decided to have a shake-up of the weekend shows, and mine was axed in favour of a pre-recorded, commercially-sponsored handbag house show presented by Boy George. It was dropped within a year.

After a few months, I found a new radio home, on Oxygen 107.9 back in Oxford, a cutting edge youth/ student station, where my mate/ club collaborator Kid Fury had already been doing an underground hip hop show called 'The Boom Box'. We started a Saturday evening one called 'Joints & Jams', and quickly found favour with management, as they gave us another slot on Thursdays.

These shows were very different to the Galaxy experience, as they were double-headers. Instantly, without any practice runs, we found we vibed excellently on air. It was generally a case of me being the straight man, holding the format of the show together, and Fury interjecting with spontaneous quips and one-liners. Like an urban Morecambe and Wise.

Oxygen was ghetto. The studios usually smelt of chips and vinegar, or McDonalds. The kettle was so caked with scale that I never saw anyone make a cup of tea in the two years I was there, and every week, a different piece of equipment would break down—usually live on air—and you'd end up with a broken dial or fader in your hand, wondering what to do. We once pre-recorded an entire show on to the station's computer 'system' as we were going to be in New York. The 'system' dumped it and our listeners got two hours of Robbie Williams and Britney Spears instead.

It was a lot of fun, though, and we got much love and very few haters. Ultimately, however, Oxygen got bought by another big radio group, and all the specialist shows fell casualty once again. Just as they always do.

CHAPTER 14

TAKE GOOD CARE OF YOURSELF

*'I really know how it feels to be stressed out, stressed out,
When you're face to face with your adversity.'*

A Tribe Called Quest Featuring Faith Evans: 'Stressed Out'
(1997)

*'What is life?
Life is like a big obstacle in front of your optical to slow
you down.
And every time you think you've gotten past it,
It's gonna come back around and tackle you to the damn
ground.'*

Eminem: 'If I Had' (1997)

DJing has its hazards. If the late nights and parties don't get you, the gout just might!

Just because we work indoors and don't have to read a Health and Safety manual, don't think there aren't some pretty hardcore health risks involved in being a DJ.

Everyday ailments aside, the obvious one that will occur to most outsiders is getting partied-out. This has never been a danger with me, as I'm a pretty clean-living guy, (some would say a lightweight.) There are others, however, who clearly struggle with such self-imposed methods of restraint.

The most legendary 'party guys', or 'caners' of the scene are house 'DJs' Brandon Block and Alex P, whose exploits mirror any of the rock and roll lifestyles exhibited by Led Zeppelin or Black Sabbath in their heyday. In early 1996, Block reacted angrily to a claim on the internet that he had died of a cocaine overdose. It turns out to have been posted by a student from Reading University on the UK Dance bulletin board, referring to his death as 'poetic justice'. Block's drug addictions certainly brought him close to death on at least one occasion, by his own admission. His most recent claim to fame was being caught on hidden TV camera negotiating a drug deal in Ibiza as recently as 2004.

A high-profile jock seen as less of a madcap loon, but whose fast living has got the better of him more than once is Carl Cox,[1] famous for playing mammoth sets at exotic locations well into the morning hours, then usually heading off to an after-party. After suffering a couple of collapses from exhaustion and a well-documented case of gout in the 90s, the big one came in Summer 2004 when he suffered a full-on heart attack. As The Big Man himself put it in an interview with the Skruff dance music website the following year:

'I'd been in Ibiza and I came back to Palma to take two days off and then get back on the circuit. My friend had got married in Ibiza, I'd done the opening for Pete Tong's

---

1. Cox took part in an NHS ad in 2021 reinforcing the official line on Covid vaccines, thus removing all doubt that he had become an Establishment stooge. See 'Musical truth Sound Bites' for an in-depth dig into his stellar career success and how he may have achieved it.

party and hadn't slept hardly at all. I'd also just done a tour of America.

'So I was constantly tired and my body system, from the point of view of my internal organs, couldn't move fast enough for what I was putting into it. My heart was pumping twice as hard to try and compensate, and in the end I had a mild heart attack.

'I also found out in hospital that I had an ulcer and a liver complaint, and now I've ended up with an irregular heartbeat, because I've also thinned out my blood. That means I've had to consciously slow my lifestyle down,[2] for my heart to be able to continue working in the right way, within its normal parameters. And forever more it's declining.'

Unpretty, huh?

Partying aside, an international DJ's gruelling schedule can be enough to take a toll on its own. A well-documented case was Danny Rampling, who famously collapsed behind the decks at London's Ministry of Sound after weeks of overdoing it, and was subsequently hospitalised and ordered by doctors to take three months off. (Danny doesn't have much luck at Ministry. Another time, he crouched down to light a fag, and in the process pulled both turntables and the mixer off their platform in front of a packed dancefloor!)

Danny recently announced his retirement from 20-plus years of professional DJing to become a restaurateur in London. His press statement explains that, as a husband

---

2. *By 2024, at which point he was well into his 60s, there was no sign whatsoever of Cox having slowed his lifestyle down, his international gig schedule just as hectic and ambitious as it had been decades before.*

and new father, the constant travel, jet lag and tiredness just no longer appeals.[3]

When the work alone can do this, it makes you wonder how the party animals cope. I once played in Glasgow on the same bill as a very well-known US house DJ. Prior to the gig, I was invited to the DJ's hotel room, where he and the promoter were hoovering up vast quantities of coke through rolled-up £50 notes.[4]

By the time he got to the gig, the DJ in question was so wasted he could barely stand, yet he still managed to put in a two-hour set, (and get paid ten times as much as I did!) After the gig, they headed straight back to the hotel for more.

It's hardly a unique case; the dance music world thrives on stories of overindulgence, with DJs boasting how long a set they can put in, (eight hours and above is nothing unusual,) and how long they can party, a feat measured in days rather than hours. Is it only a matter of time before these characters come undone, or are they just made of stronger stuff than me? I don't know.

When I worked alongside Graham Gold in radio in the early 90s, he used to regale me with his stories of lifestyle excesses—usually mad dashes around the UK covering two or three gigs in a night, arriving back in London just hours before his weekend Kiss FM shows, which used to go out around midday. I saw him as quite an inspiration, (and he was pushing 40 even then!)

To try and emulate his energy, at least in part, I developed a habit of downing gallons of coffee, hoping for the sort of buzz that could keep me going through long

---

3. *Spoiler alert—it didn't work.*

4. *And that DJ was... no, it wouldn't be fair!*

hours and late nights. Didn't really work. Just used to just make me drive like a lunatic.

I'm not alone there. It's often DJs that will proudly give you stories of how quickly they've gotten from A to B when properly fired up. I once accepted a lift to my radio show in Bristol from a long-standing DJ mate from Oxford, who for the purposes of this story we'd better call Mr. X! He'd just juiced an absurd amount of money on a slick new sports car that apparently went like shit off a shovel, and was keen to show me the evidence.

I only realised my mistake when I found myself being pressed back into the seat by centrifugal force and looking like Roger Moore in 'Moonraker,' my skin rippling across my face and my knuckles as white as this page. Meanwhile, X nonchalantly tickled the steering wheel with one hand, and rolled a spliff on his lap with the other. We got there in 42 minutes. When I tell you Abingdon to Bristol is approximately 80 miles, you'll see the point!

Another of my DJ friends, (Mr. Y!,) told me of a chemically-fuelled drive he and a club manager made back from the Brixton Fridge early one morning. If I remember correctly, it was the far end of the M25 to the Oxford Ring Road in 20 minutes—a distance of just over 40 miles. It's *just about* possible. (This was in the days before speed cameras, by the way—not that there are any on the M40 even now.)

While not quite as impressive statistically, a few of my own road trips have been pretty efficient. Newcastle to Oxfordshire in three hours? Leeds in two? These are all done in the wee small hours, of course, and tend to be fuelled by nothing more than a steely determination to get home to the comfort of my own bed before the sun comes up. That and the occasional can of Red Bull. (Don't under-estimate this stuff. My brother-in-law once drank three cans straight. He couldn't sleep for two days.)

Prior to that it was all about Pro Plus, large quantities of caffeine condensed into little white pills—the only sort I used to pop. I'd dissolve them in my mouth rather than swallowing them, somehow hoping to increase their potency. They tasted absolutely foul. As a modern-day alternative, my wife recently presented me with a set of 'caffeine strips'. They're like rice paper, and dissolve into a nasty-tasting paste when you chew them. But they do seem to give you a kick!

It was in my Pro Plus era that I became almost addicted to knackeredness, and I wasn't satisfied until I'd pushed myself to the bounds of my physical limitations. I think the logic was that if you feel constantly exhausted, it's a sign that you're wringing every last drop out of life, and really achieving everything you can.

I followed my DJ heroes a little too closely in the early days, frequently coming close to collapse through sleep neglect, and basically doing too much. I was naively overlooking the fact that, unlike me, these guys were probably getting their buzz from a little more than natural energy.

When it comes to sleep, by default, DJs' patterns give cause for concern at the best of times. Different jocks cope with the strains in different ways. Many simply become totally nocturnal, never going to bed before the sun comes up,[5] and then not stirring until way into the afternoon. (Ever tried to get Cardiff's Vibe 101 DJ Raheem on the phone before 3pm? Forget it.)[6]

---

5. Me in the late 90s. I have a different problem now. I can only generally sleep between the hours of 11pm and 7am.

6. R.I.P. Raheem.

When I was a bachelor, this suited me fine. Since getting married, however, I've pulled myself back into the land of the morning-risers in an attempt to maintain some semblance of a normal existence. I've even been known to get up with the missus at 7am and put in a full day's work! I find it quite cathartic.

The only way I cope now is through a method that I discovered a few years ago, and which has been working highly successfully for me ever since—the Disco Nap! These are virtually essential in the case of gruelling overseas travel schedules, but they work equally well on any day where I need a boost of energy for an upcoming late night. I now consider myself to have the ability to look anywhere between 18 and 40 years of age, depending entirely on how much sleep I've achieved. Even a quick snooze of 90 minutes can work wonders in restoring strength, energy and appearance. I was encouraged to hear my doctor endorse this quite recently. He said even closing your eyes for an hour is almost as effective as the same time spent asleep.[7]

I think it's pretty much down to individuals, though. Many people—my wife among them—complain they feel so groggy after waking from such a short sleep, that they end up in a worse state than if they'd stayed up. All I know is it works for me.

It's surprising how quickly you stir from a state of knackeredness when it's time to step behind the decks and do your thing. I've staggered into gigs so fatigued I can barely stand, only to receive an instant boost of energy to carry me buzzing through my two-hour set. Big up adrenalin!

---

[7]. *Disco naps served me very well right up to the onset of the Covid nonsense in early 2020. Since then it's been a physical impossibility for me to sleep during the day.*

But it can be a curse too. Many's the time I've headed to my hotel room after a show, desperate to grab the three or four hours of limited sleep that I'm afforded before having to get up again for a morning flight. It takes so damn long to wind down, you can easily spend two hours just lying there waiting for the buzz to wear off. There are few sounds in the world more frustrating than an alarm clock ringing just thirty minutes after you've nodded off.

The historical record will show that famous DJs' lifestyles and marriage don't generally mix. Of the high-profile UK DJs who've tied the knot over the past decade or so, there are only a handful that are still together. (Norman Cook and Zoe only *just* made it!)[8]

Time away from home and punishing work schedules are factors. Random birds, groupies and DJ shaggers can be, too, (so I'm told.) But so is the passion and love that successful DJs inevitably have for their work. In some cases, it can all add up to such buzz and excitement, that poor old wifey/ hubby at home can just no longer compete.

A tragic variation on this was the news that a former radio station Programme Controller of mine, who was also one of the station's key presenters, committed suicide a few months after being axed from his high-profile position. He could no longer cope with not having the status he'd got used to enjoying. Seems a bit of a harsh measure considering it was only local radio, but just goes to show how a DJ's job can truly eclipse all else in their assessment of life's priorities. (He had a wife and kids, too.)

A recurring peril of the job is flying. I'm not sure being cooped up in a pressurised capsule full of recycled air and passing through multiple time zones in a matter of hours was much of a factor when human beings were first designed. A DJ friend of mine from the West Midlands did

---

8. *Spoiler alert—it didn't last!*

so much flying on a recent trip to the States, that it actually triggered a form of epilepsy, and he was hospitalised for weeks.

I can sympathise. My 2005 visit to Malaysia, Australia and New Zealand threw up some pretty hardcore statistics: six cities in three countries with three different time zones in nine days; a flight a day for eight consecutive days, equating to a total of 52 hours in the skies; somewhere around 31,000 miles covered. Michael Palin and Phileas Fogg, step aside!

You might even take a beating in this job. The records and gear that DJs tote are highly valuable, and many a casualty has taken a slap after walking into the wrong street at the wrong time of night. I can only claim to have been a victim to this once, and I'm rather embarrassed to say it was by a girl.

I was leaving a ghetto spot on the wrong side of Coventry, not having had a particularly great night on account of the promoter attempting to stitch me up. All that was on my mind was getting home. As I exited, a 'girl', having evidently been ejected by the door staff, ran up to me with fire in her eyes, screaming and waving her hands around in a frenzy. She'd seemingly mistaken me for one of the doormen.

The poor cow was obviously deluded. Me, a doorman?! I forget my actual response, but it was something along the lines of 'fuck off'. (It had been a hard night, you understand.) This didn't go down too well, and I got a blinding punch to the centre of the face as a result.

What can you do? A guy hitting a girl is socially unacceptable, so I couldn't lash back, (though, trust me, the instinct was strong.) And if I'd got into a fracas and the police had arrived, which of us would be liable to be thrown into a cell to cool off for the night? I just wish my wife had been with me. It would have been the catfight of the century!

DJing is more likely than most other professions to irreparably damage your hearing. This was the premise of the 2005 movie 'It's All Gone Pete Tong', where Paul Kaye plays Frankie Wilde, a hard-living Ibiza jock who loses his hearing after years of standing next to blasting monitor speakers and having his headphone volume cranked, Spinal Tap-like, to number 11.

The movie was a comical treatment, but with its touching moments, rightly asserting that there's nothing really funny about being deaf by the age of 40. This has been recognised by the nightlife game, which now markets trendy, but ultra-expensive earplugs designed for use in clubs, to limit the amount of noise intake.

But despite all these perils, the most major potential risk to a DJ's health and general well-being is one that's hardly ever considered, but is statistically more likely to maim or kill than anything else.

Smoking.

Following years of playing in clubs so smoke-drenched that you can barely see six feet in front of you, one of my most striking experiences was the time I walked into a club shortly after New York's State-wide ban on smoking in public places. The clean atmosphere made an impact immediately, and the luxury of leaving with my clothes and hair *not* smelling like an overflowing ashtray was quite incredible.[9]

---

9. *It's been so long since smoking has been allowed in inside venues that it's hard to remember that stinking grey fog used to be a given when stepping inside any bar or club.*

Tales from the Flipside

Since then, various countries have followed the New York/ California[10] ban, Ireland, Italy and New Zealand among them. Scotland has already experimented with a partial ban, and the rest of the UK is finally set to follow in Spring 2007.

Prior to the announcement, England's policy was all a bit of a shambles. For some reason, the city of Liverpool first stood out on its own in trying to take action. Then a partial ban was proposed, covering only those venues which serve food.[11] That would have meant nightclubs not being affected at all.

In Ireland, desperate smokers now congregate outside the venue's front door, (assuming the club is gracious enough to allow them back in afterwards.) The resulting concentrated haze is now a new obstacle for departing non-smoking punters to overcome!

In my website forum debate on this subject, my DJ friend Drew Myrie didn't disappoint with his input. His user name is 'Don Juan', but I think of him more as 'Devil's Advocate'!

'I never enjoy going home stinking of cigarettes. It's a nasty smell and doesn't exactly stir the oils of passion at the end of the night, (if you know what I mean!). But isn't smoking is an inherent part of this side of society? People who don't like the smoky pub atmosphere, just don't go to smoky pubs.

And surely pubs/ clubs supply what people want—if they'd got it wrong they'd soon be out of business, right? Anyone who thinks it's that important to ban smoking in 'clubland' should put their hand in the pocket and open a

---

10. *The "woke"-ism was clearly creeping into those leftist states even back then.*

11. *An early dry run for Covid??*

venue based on these health-conscious ethics. If it worked, this would have a much greater effect on the industry. As is evident, the lawmakers can't even make up their minds, so what we will end up with is a half-arsed attempt that doesn't work anyway.'

The long-running UK clubbers' magazine 'Mixmag' conducted a survey among their readership in late '04, with 70 per cent agreeing that smoking should be banned in pubs and clubs—a much higher percentage than I'd have thought, given that Mixmag's readers tend to be hardened party-goers who like to have a good time.

A possible smoking ban on customers is one thing. What about the DJs it would affect? I personally know scores of chainies who might be forced to seek alternative career paths if they couldn't have their beloved fag in their mouth while they play. (And if this were America, that last phrase would have an entirely different meaning!)

2007. A new era.

CHAPTER 15

JOCKING ALL OVER THE WORLD, PART 3

*'Same song. I'm back. Been around the world,
Romancing girls that dance with girls.
From Club Cheetah to Club Amnesia,
Dabena's in LA, bubblin' in Dublin.'*
Jay-Z: 'I Just Wanna Love You' (2000)

*'I bang cock in Bangkok
Can't stop, I turn and hit the same spot.
Think not. I'm the thriller in Manilla
Schlong in Hong Kong.'*

Ludacris:' Area Codes' (2001)

*'Mami, mamasita, have you ever
Flown on G5s. From London, to Ibiza?
You'll have sundaes with chiquitas.
You'll see Venus and Serena, in the Wimbledon Arena.'*

Snoop Dogg: 'Signs' (2004)

Mark Devlin

Rising Damp in Derry, The Exorcist in Prague, and Midnight Express in Romania.

You take things a stage at a time on an overseas assignment. With the flight and the transfer out of the way, the next step is to wonder whether the alleged hotel reservation has actually been made. When the promoter's with you, it's not a problem, but when you've made your own way there, it's anybody's guess.

The amount of times I've given my name at a reception desk, only to get the soul-crushing response, 'no, no, there's no booking under that name at all' cannot be measured. It's either that, or the promoter has misunderstood the booking procedure, and has only *reserved* a room on their credit card rather than paid for it. Then, the hotel won't let you take the room unless you let them swipe your credit card, and you have to hope and pray you can get the guy to give you your money back.

Most of the time, the hotels you get laid on are fine. Although things like 24-hour room service and in-house internet access are always good, the only requirements I really have are the very basic ones; a clean, comfortable bed, a quiet room, air con. in the case of warm countries, and a shower. That's it. After all, your time spent there is often very limited. It's like the rock star memoirs you read, where they complain that, far from being glamorous, life on the road is actually just a non-stop barrage of airports, taxis and hotels.

Even with such humble standards as mine you can be disappointed. When a nightclub in Northern Ireland asked me if I'd mind staying a 'guest house', rather than the 'hotel' I'd stipulated, I was happy to save them a few quid. What I got was a fleapit that was probably in worst condition than the average borstal. It was the sort of place where you don't want to take off your shoes for fear of dirtying your socks on the carpet.

I stayed in a similar spot in Brighton a couple of years later, and this time there was no-one else to blame. I'd just started going out with my girlfriend, Parveen, and decided to take her on what was intended to be a romantic weekend.

It pissed down all day and night, and we arrived to find every last room in town had been taken... except one. It was in a house very similar to the one mentioned above, and, despite it being 11pm and with no further hope of him shifting the room, the landlord still charged us full whack.

Parveen ended up getting a migraine, and the only thing we heard all night was the couple in the next room going at it like rabbits, and the girl squealing like a pig. The morning after, we peeked in their room to find it had a four-poster bed. Ours was a grimy mattress on a busted base. It was not good.

With all the potential hassle of leaving it to chance, sometimes it's better to take care of the hotel booking yourself. It was on a visit to Prague that I decided to combine a gig with an extended break for Parveen and myself. It turned out to be highly memorable as the only time I believe I've had a supernatural experience.[1]

Prague is a fascinating city with a character all of its own, and steeped in history. Some of it's very grim, however, and the tone for the night seemed to have been set when we visited a medieval torture museum—very macabre stuff.

For our last night in town, we'd taken the advice of my DJ mate Stretch Taylor. He recommended what was basically a lavish restaurant, set on a hillside overlooking the old city, and only accessible by a type of cable car. Above the restaurant are two suites, which the venue lets out to customers. Ours consisted of a plush lounge complete

---

1. But there have been a few more since.

with its own billiards table, then a bedroom with a grand four-poster bed.

Over dinner, a strange bearded guy at the piano who looked a bit like Benny from ABBA started giving us very unsettling looks. But we let it go.

Some time around 3am,[2] I awoke to the sound of an abrupt, hollow knock somewhere outside our room.[3] A few minutes later, I felt a hand touch my shoulder. I rolled over to see what Parveen wanted—but she was several inches out of reach on the other side of the bed. Then the noises started; a strange chanting and a kind of whimpering, plus the sound of footsteps pacing around above. The air turned cold, and there was a very strange atmosphere.

The next morning, we noticed a spiral staircase leading up from the lobby to a black door and a type of loft above our room. At breakfast, we saw a selection of highly macabre paintings, depicting what looked like torture scenes and classical visions of hell.[4] Benny was there at checkout, smiling.

We left. Quickly.

When I relayed the tale, Stretch couldn't stop laughing. Admittedly, I'd have probably done the same, as I'm not

---

2. 3am has long been known as "the witching hour"—the time when the fabric between the "physical" CD world and the spiritual one is at its thinnest, allowing for the most interaction between the two.

3. Actually, on reflection, it was three knocks in short succession—a standard satanist's calling card and inspiration for the song 'Knock Three Times,' itself identified as a trigger in trauma-based mind-control programming.

4. Have there ever been more blatant clues as to a venue's true nature as a haven and hotbed for dark occultists? And have I ever been more naïve at any point in my life than I evidently was then?!

normally one for this type of stuff. But there was definitely something going on!⁵

You're never guaranteed a noise-free environment in hotels, and this can be a real pain the ass when you want to catch a power nap, often essential in preparing for an all-night gig. There's a hotel I stay at in Germany which I'm convinced has a sideline as a knocking shop, as I only ever hear headboards banging against the wall.

There was one in Kristiansand, Norway, where the sound of seagulls was so loud, even through double glazing, that there was no chance of rest. (The entire building was caked from top to bottom in birdshit, to give an idea of their numbers!) We got so pissed off with a bunch of rowdy English (what else?!) thugs in an adjoining room in Cape Town, that it was a blessing when their weed smoke started drifting under the door, as we had the perfect excuse to get them evicted and enjoy some quiet—which we did.

But sometimes flight schedules are such that it's not even feasible to take a hotel room at all. There have been a few occasions where I've taken the last flight of the day out to some European spot, then the dawn flight back in the morning, for reasons of economy. This results in going straight from the club back to the airport, and sometimes waiting around for two or three hours for the check-in desks to open. It's a good idea not to have drunk too much on such occasions, or you're liable to fall asleep on a bench and miss your flight.

After one such occasion in Stuttgart, I was horrified to be dropped at the airport to find my flight back to Heathrow had been totally cancelled due to bad weather—particularly as I was due to fly to Edinburgh later that day for another gig which couldn't be missed. I ended up having to take the next flight to Birmingham, the only

---

5. *No shit, Sherlock.*

point of entry into the UK that was open, then make my way back to Heathrow via another expensive combination of trains, taxis and buses, just to retrieve my car.

Of all my years of travel, one day in particular surpasses all others as The Nightmare Day Direct From The Bowels Of Hell. This was the day where it took me from 8.30am CET to just after midnight GMT to travel from Ibiza to my front door in England—a distance of little more than 900 miles. In that time, sixteen and a half hours, I could have flown from London to Tokyo with time to spare, or three quarters of the way to Australia. And it was all down to a dopey hotel receptionist.

After returning my hire car to the airport in comfortable time for my 10.15am flight home, I was mortified to realise that my hotel back in San Antonio had failed to give me back my passport when I'd checked out. By the time I'd driven back to get it, my flight was long gone, and my options were looking grim.

There's an appalling lack of direct services from Ibiza to London,[6] and the only one for the rest of the day left a couple of hours later. There was myself and a couple of other guys on standby. One of them turned out to be James Lavelle, DJ and founder of the Mo Wax label, and a fellow Oxford head, who'd already missed two flights home.

Three people on standby. Two seats available. Guess who got left behind? It turned out my only other option was to spend £150 on a brand new ticket to go with Air Berlin. The flight didn't leave for seven hours, and even then it wasn't direct, having to route via Palma Mallorca. And it was delayed—obviously.

All this occurred to me following two exceptionally late nights, with only two hours sleep under my belt, and a

---

6. *Many more now, thankfully, including direct BA services from Heathrow. But not back in the early 2000s.*

day after an Ibiza pizzeria had forcibly retained my watch while I went off to find some cash to settle my bill after discovering that they don't take payment by credit card.[7] Days like these unfold like some absurd comedy movie, but they're really not too funny while they're happening! You often find yourself questioning the nature of your job at such times.

As a globetrotting DJ with journalistic tendencies, it was inevitable that I'd start to feel like a travelogue writer before long. So since I'm on the subject of adventurous overseas experiences, although this one wasn't a DJing trip, it really wouldn't be right to miss out on my recent encounters in Romania.

The embarrassing thing about it is that Mrs. D and myself actually went there as part of our Honeymoon. I'd been hoodwinked by a skilfully criminal piece of marketing by the Romanian Tourist Board into believing it was an enchanting place to visit, and that it was a world away from the repressed, bankrupt Communist state we saw on our TV screens in the 80s.

At the time of booking, we were feeling adventurous. Plus Parveen was gassed up by the legend of Count Dracula, based on the real-life Vlad The Impaler,[8] and wanted to see Bran Castle where he lived.

What we weren't prepared for was the fact that, even fifteen years after the fall of communism and the ousting of the Ceaucescu Regime, Romania is still outrageously poor

---

7. *There's no way I'd settle for that nonsense these days!*

8. *Since gleefully revealed by Prince/ "King" Charles, aka Lord Sausage Fingers, as having been a distant ancestor on his mother's side.*

and run-down.[9] Crazily, the one thing that the country has going for it in terms of a potential tourist attraction, ie the Dracula legend, is played down to such a degree that there's hardly any trace of it when you get there. The result is an absolute zero concept of tourist relations, despite what the Board might try and convince you to the contrary!

Our entry into the country was via a seven-hour train journey from Hungary, on what resembled a toilet on wheels. In fact, the actual toilet was literally a hole in the ground leading on to the tracks! It eventually terminated in crumbling Cluj Napoca, in the Northern part of Transylvania. From there, we hired a car to drive down to the city of Brasov, much further South.

Driving in Romania is an acquired skill. The general rule seems to be to overtake first, and only then to worry if there's a dirty great juggernaut bearing down on you. If that doesn't get you, the crater-sized potholes just might, especially if you're swerving to avoid one of the hundreds of donkey carts.

Romanian 'cuisine' is equally distinctive. Specialities include polenta, made from maize, which is served with anything and everything, plus the delightfully tempting options of brain and tripe, which also appear on every menu.

After three days, we were more than ready to board the return train. This was where the real drama began.

A few miles from the Hungarian border, the train stopped in the middle of nowhere. Before long, our carriage was swarming with an army of police and customs officials, and our passports were swiftly seized for a 'check'. Next, a police officer came into our carriage, told us to

---

9. *As the backdrop for the run-down, backward Kazakhstan village of the narrative in his 'Borat' movie, Sacha Baron-Cohen reportedly filmed in an even more run-down village in Romania.*

stand up, and lifted our seats to look underneath. By this time, the words 'stitch-up' and some chilling recollections of 'Midnight Express' were filling my mind. It also turned out that, due to language confusion, we didn't have valid tickets for our journey.

Mercifully, our passports were eventually handed back, and a quick backhander ensured the ticket inspector stayed off our backs. After what felt like an eternity, the train eventually pulled up in Budapest.

We went out and got very drunk. On the way back, we passed a subway station, from which the echoey sounds of The Clash's 'Rock The Kasbah' were bellowing. Going down to investigate, we found a lively freestyle DJ party in full effect in one of the subterranean walkways.

The tune was one I'd heard a hundred times before, but it just sounded so fresh and exciting in this context. Maybe it was all down to the relief of having survived our ordeal, or the atmospheric surroundings. Hearing other DJs play tunes that I myself would probably choose not to, and the songs sounding really great is something I've experienced many other times, too, and it adds weight to the popular idea that a good DJ really is putting in a bona-fide performance, rather than just mindlessly slapping on a few records.

CHAPTER 16

THE ENEMY WITHIN

'Don't waste your time with jealousy. Sometimes you're ahead, sometimes you're behind. The race is long. But in the end, it's only with yourself.'

Baz Luhrmann: 'Everybody's Free To Wear Sunscreen' (1999)

'They say it's lonely at the top, and whatever you do, You always gotta watch muthafuckas around you.'

Gang Starr: 'Moment Of Truth' (1998)

*'What are friends?
Friends are people that you think are your friends.
But they're really your enemies with secret identities,
What is money?
Money will make those same friends come back around
Swearing they was always down.'*

Eminem: 'If I Had' (1998)

'Don't watch me—watch TV!'

Juelz Santana: 'Mic Check 1,2' (2005)

Tales from the Flipside

In any profession that gets groupies, it's only to be expected there'll be a few haters to help balance things out.

Read any inside account of life in the Hollywood film industry—Peter Biskind's 'Easy Riders, Raging Bulls' or Julia Philips' 'You'll Never Eat Lunch In This Town Again' are great examples—and you get the lowdown on just how much jealousy, bitterness and rivalry there is in the movie game. There's so many tantrums, power games and stabs in the back, it makes you wonder how films ever get made at all!

It's pretty much the same in the pop/ rock music world.[1] The never-ending beefs between hip hop artists speak for themselves. And, as any Fleet Street hack will tell you, there's more of the same in journalism.

The average anthropologist would probably tell you that the way we humans interact instinctively with each other is just as fascinating as any wildlife documentary. If you're looking for a profession to get an insight into many aspects of the human psyche, therefore, you could leave aside any of the above and try DJs instead.

We tend to be a jealous, confrontational and fiercely competitive bunch, and many DJs seem to draw perverted pleasure from making others' rides as bumpy as possible. When it's not this, it's down to irrational insecurity, or simply a primal instinct for survival by seeing off one's rivals.

Anyway, I used to take such matters quite to heart, judging by the inner sleeve note on my very first mixtape:

---

1. Little did I realise at the time that, of course it's going to be that way given that both institutions—and all others in Organised Society—are ultimately controlled by the very same forces.

'To all the stoopid playa-haters and the jealous bitch-a*s muthaf*ckas out there. Thanks for the negativity—while it's consuming you, it's inspiring me. To all the narrow-minded bigots that refuse to accept the power of this music. One day you'll understand.'

Hmmm. I'll accept the suggestion that I may have been a little over-sensitive in those days. But the point about other people's negativity spurring you on is a valid one. Hate is a motivating factor. It's summed up by the outro voicer on Funkmaster Flex's first '60 Minutes Of Funk' mix album from 1996:

'For those of you who don't support me and don't like me, I appreciate it very much. 'Cos your negative vibes makes me get up that much earlier in the morning. Thank you!'

Word up!

When you're on top, you're hated and loved in equal measure. The only way to deal with it is to be realistic, and consider that hating is actually a form of flattery. It shows you matter, it shows you stand out, and it shows you're having an effect. It's telling that, whenever the dance or urban music press run polls on DJs, Judge Jules and Tim Westwood tend to top both the most and the least favourite DJ sections. In the same polls![2]

To experience many of the subtle ways in which DJ rivalry exhibits itself, you don't have to look any further than the booth.

There's a kind of etiquette when it comes to one DJ handing over the decks to another; it's all unspoken, but it's a code of civilised conduct that's generally understood.

---

2. *Also telling that, all these years on, I've finally come to recognise these as the appointed gatekeepers of their respective scenes, so the question of who hates or who loves them really is neither here nor there!*

Tales from the Flipside

For instance, it's good manners to let the previous DJ's final track play for a reasonable length of time before storming in with your own. An ignorant DJ will stop a tune dead after thirty seconds, his ego goading him on to announce himself as quickly as possible. Like the crowd cares.

It's at change-over point that plain sabotage can occur. I've known other DJs deliberately turn down bass and treble controls, re-assign crossfaders on the mixer, and loosen styluses immediately before I've been due to take over. The intention is to cause me to fuck up on my first record, making me look technically inept, and setting off bad vibes for the rest of my set.

It's incredible how many supposedly professional DJs will resort to such childish pettiness, often over something as trivial as the next man being given a better set time than them, or higher billing on the flyer. Fortunately, I've learned to spot most of the tricks.

These are coward moves. Others can be more blatant. In some of the rawer ghetto spots I've played, the next DJ has announced his arrival by forcibly barging me out of the booth with a six-strong crew, and practically hurling my record box to the floor so he can put his own down.

I've had my fair share of jibes and insults over the years. When you're a white DJ playing 'black' music you can always expect the odd slur. But most of the negativity I've had to deal with has come from the way my peers have behaved.

An unmistakable way of identifying hostility comes from what I call 'hovering DJ syndrome.' This phenomenon, which will be familiar to most travelling DJs, occurs when a guest arrives and tears up a spot, and the resident DJ can't handle it and desperately wants to get back on the decks, like a spoilt child. You know this is happening when all you can see in the corner of your eye is the guy anxiously hovering, (because female jocks don't do it,) headphones and record in hand, bouncing up and down like he wants to go to the toilet.

As far as I'm concerned, if you can't master the etiquette, get out of the game. It's all part of being a professional.

The worst offender has been a snidey little snake DJ with whom I've had the misfortune of sharing a few bills when I've been out in Johannesburg.

Having my mixes broadcast regularly on national radio has helped me become a bit of a DJ celeb in South Africa, and this tends to lead to good receptions in clubs. The first time I span alongside the snake, it was clear he wasn't secure enough to handle this, and all the tricks detailed above were used.

On the third occasion, he told me the promoter had switched our agreed set times, and that he was now playing before me, due to finish at 3am. I sensed foul play, but frankly, couldn't be bothered to argue, getting paid being my only real priority. I walked into the room at the agreed time to find no music, an empty dancefloor and the snake scuttling away with his CDs, and taunting 'where are your crowd now, big man?!' I found it necessary to explain to him what a bitch he was, which his mates seemed to find hilarious. Our paths have thankfully never crossed since.

The truth is, we're all prone to feel a certain animosity towards bigger DJs, but the professional way is not to let it show. For my own part, the only hint of this arises when I'm sharing a billing with some hot shot or other, and the promoter tries to screw me down on my fee in order to pay the absurdly over-stated one the high-flier is demanding. Perhaps not the best way to get the most out of your supporting performers!

Tales from the Flipside

There's an even more underhand tactic towards pissing off your fellow DJ, however. It's one that first came to light in the mid 90s when the Inland Revenue suddenly became aware of the vast salaries that certain DJs were earning. Ours is a cash-in-hand business, and tipping off the Tax Office that a certain DJ may not be declaring all his tax earnings became the new bitch move.

In 2002, I fell victim to this myself. A dusty old tax clerk reminiscent of Captain Mainwaring from Dad's Army contacted me out of the blue saying he wished to make enquiries into my 1999/ 2000 tax return. It's the bureaucratic equivalent of being pulled by the police for a roadside 'routine check.'

Anyone that's ever had one of these will tell you they're about as much fun as toothache. Mainwaring had got it into his silver head that *all* DJs are high-flying, drug-taking, party-loving criminals, sitting on vast hordes of illegally-acquired cash, and not declaring any of it. Not only was I required to dig out all my receipts, bank and credit card statements and cheque book stubs from the period, I was also questioned as to what I ate, drank and smoked, where I shopped for clothes, and how many pairs of shoes I bought in a year!

Fortunately, I'm indebted to my good friend Dave Morrison, who, as well as being a retired soul/ R&B DJ, also happens to earn his living as an accountant. This made him ideal as my representative. I almost felt sorry for the bureaucrat, being on the receiving end of Dave's characteristic dry wit. In one of his letters was the glaring literal 'to be pacific, I would like further information on . . . ', which drew Dave's response: 'I'm not entirely clear on how the world's largest ocean fits into this discussion. Perhaps you could elaborate?'

In the end, I can't imagine how many man hours of the Inland Revenue's time the 'investigation' took. The Captain wasted at least three days questioning my use of the phrase 'door tax' in my website gig listings. 'Aha', he clearly thought, 'now I've got him!' . . . not realising that door tax is clubland slang for the admission price.

There was a slight irregularity in my figures, however, and it turned out I owed the revenue sixty quid. Not quite sure it justified eighteen months of ongoing correspondence, but there you go.

If you judge your success by your ability to get other people's backs up, then I hit the big time when I recently managed to achieve my very own 'mystery' hater, who attempted to embark on an ongoing e-mail campaign.

One day, I logged into my e-mails to find one attributed to one 'Sanjay Gupta', probably the most obvious made-up name in history. The guy had been looking at my website, and seemed to be trying to rip the piss out of me for portraying myself as some kind of bad boy or gangster.[3]

Unfortunately, the poor devil had missed the mark by about a thousand miles. I've never attempted to portray myself in this way. I'm just a guy trying to make a go of things in his chosen profession, and the way that I market myself is directly related to the type of music I play, and the circles in which I move. 'Sanjay' tried too hard to be intellectual and ironic, and just got the whole thing wrong. I think he'd been reading *'The Guardian.'*

At first, I was offended. But very soon, this turned to a feeling of flattery when I considered the trouble this guy had gone to. First of all, he'd set up a Hotmail account

---

3. *To be fair, looking back now with the benefit of hindsight and maturity, I can't actually blame him. I wouldn't like the me of back then now!*

specially attributed to the hilarious Sanjay Gupta. Imagine the hassle.

Secondly, he attempted to disguise his true identity by telling me he ran an Indian restaurant in Glasgow, then actually went to the trouble of looking in Directory Enquiries so he could mail me the number of a bona-fide one to throw me off track. (A curious research call confirmed that of course there was no Sanjay Gupta working there.)

A few weeks later, he mailed again, this time having assembled a specially doctored picture of me extracted from my website. Just how unstable do you have to be to do this? The real irony is that this guy is attempting to discredit me, and he's the one with such an empty aimless life that he's got time to actually bother with such nonsense. Personally, I couldn't be arsed. So I just ignored him, which is the best thing you can do.

It soon became a bit of a detective game in terms of trying to pinpoint who this wacko really was, because it was obviously somebody I already knew. It didn't take long to work out. So if you're reading this, 'Sanjay', you've been sussed. And the great thing is, you'll never actually be certain whether I *really* know it's you![4]

What I find curious is that I'm not even famous, so what the hell do the big shots have to put up with? Or maybe it's more subtle at that level?

For my own part, I just see myself as a very focused, very determined and very persistent guy, and it's through these qualities that I've achieved what I have. I've had very few lucky breaks, and I've never had anything handed to me on a plate.

---

4. Actually, I never was 100 per cent on who it could have been, but thought that line in the book would convince whoever the culprit was that I absolutely was.

So if you've worked hard for what you have, why should you be resented for it? The people that hate you tend to be the ones incapable of doing stuff for themselves, so that breeds their contempt towards those who do.

I guess it'll always be that way.

CHAPTER 17

DJ NIGHTMARES

'And all your dreams are like a horror flick of Stephen King'
Fugees: 'Nappyhead' (Remix) (1994)

'Man, don't you know this would be worse than Stephen King's 'Misery'
Big Daddy Kane on Heavy D & The Boyz: 'Don't Curse' (1991)

At least once in most DJs' careers, the job takes you to a very dark place.[1]

Being an astronaut or a train driver is the dream of many a six year-old. By the time they're sixteen, the dream may well have changed to being a DJ. It's an appealing profession for many excitable young music fans, and given the public perception of the lavish party lifestyles that DJs seem to enjoy, it's not hard to understand why.

In a cruel twist of irony that life tends to very good at throwing up, however, the opposite is very often true. The well-meaning pursuit of playing tunes for a living can lead

---

1. *The same, it turns out, can be said for researchers!*

to some pretty horrendous nightmare scenarios. The sort of thing you'd really prefer not to have to go through.

On reflection, I guess I can consider myself pretty lucky in this department. Although I've had my fair share of what you might call off-key situations, when it comes to fully-fledged horror stories, I've fared pretty well. I spent a while trying to recall my single most nightmarish gig, and it might *not* actually be the New Year's Eve farce detailed in chapter one. I think it might have to be the time I was lured up to Preston by a DJ I vaguely knew.

The agreement was that the venue provide a fixed DJ fee and a hotel for the night. Now, I'm no prima donna when it comes to accommodation—a clean comfortable bed and a shower in the morning does me fine. I should have smelt a rat when I pulled up at the venue to find the 'manageress' leaping into my car and asking me to give her a lift across town, before going on to my 'hotel.'

The 'hotel' in question was what we in hip hop call 'roach', and looked like a cross between Rigsby's house in 'Rising Damp' and Ronnie Barker's cell in 'Porridge'. The 'receptionist' looked like Phil Mitchell in a string vest, sipping a can of lager behind the 'desk' and taking care to scratch his arse before handing me the key.[2] The 'manageress' was acting very sketchy and couldn't wait to dive off, so I very quickly asked Mitchell if the room had been pre-paid, as it should have been. It wasn't, so I grabbed the 'manageress' before she jetted and frogmarched her back in to pay for the 'room', suspecting further foul play to come.

I got it. The 'club' was basically an empty shell, and it was clear than no promotion had been done on the night whatsoever. The fact that there were ten people in

---

2. *Memories of Mel Smith's receptionist character in 'National Lampoon's European Vacation' spring to mind.*

attendance and that five of them were staff was the first giveaway. (The other five were gangster types lurking around the edges smoking weed.) The sound 'system' was on its last legs, making the music sound like it was being filtered through a sock. I became very suspicious before the end of the night when no-one from 'management' could be found, and sure enough, they'd done a runner. My DJ contact promised to follow things up for me the next day. Yeah, right.

What really took the piss about this most monumental of stitch-ups was the fact that the venue clearly had no intention of paying me from the off, and had no problem with the knowledge that I'd driven 180 miles at my own expense, and given them several hours of my not unimportant time. But not only that, had I not forced the 'manageress' to come back and pay from the 'room', they'd have quite happily let me be saddled with the bill for that as well.

I considered driving home, but I was too tired, so three or four hours' sleep at Porridge Towers it had to be. The 'room' was the sort where you opt to sleep in your clothes for fear of being eaten alive by bedbugs. 'Breakfast' was populated entirely by truckers, navvies and cons, all in uniform grubby string vests and tucking into plates of lard.

I spent the following weeks leaning heavily into my DJ contact to get my pay—not unreasonable, I felt, considering he was the guy that endorsed the booking. A cheque eventually arrived. It bounced.

I had another, far more reliable DJ friend in the North at the time, who said he would have been quite happy to go down the venue with a couple of mates and forcibly extract the money for me...had he not just been banged up for a year for possession of firearms. Like you do. (He got out recently, and walked immediately back into three new DJing gigs a week, no questions asked. Not many professions where you could achieve that.)

Sounds pretty dire, right? I thought it was. Until I started looking into other DJs' worst gig experiences, and it became very clear that many have suffered much greater misfortunes than me...so far, at least.

In 2005, the UK publication Mixmag surveyed a handful of prominent DJs on their worst ever gig experiences.

Xpress 2 were due to play a festival in Acapulco, but fate had other ideas. They ended up missing their connecting flights, losing their luggage and spending six hours in the back of a van. They missed their slot at the festival, and found the hotel had no reservations. The following day they woke up to a storm with knee-level water, and heard the festival site had been completely washed away.

Smokin' Jo arrived at a club to find a guy staggering out with blood all over his face, and rough-looking gangsters in the corner doing crack. As soon as she started playing, the crackheads started leaning over the decks, scratching her records, and generally giving her a whole load of grief.

Then the promoter failed to pay her.

Progressive house DJ Steve Lawler had been playing at a club in Guadalajara, Mexico, when the owner insisted he play a 15-minute trance record called 'Dance With The Devil'.[3] His refusal didn't go down too well. When he tried to leave, ten bouncers came over and threatened to beat the shit out of him. He was forced back into the club and made to play for another hour surrounded by the knuckleheads.

Hard dance DJ BK tells of a gig in South Africa that got stormed by police. He knew about this when he turned around from the booth to find an officer with a machine

---

3. *Certainly sounds like he was in the wrong kind of gig!*

gun behind him. The police proceeded to look through all his records, putting most back in the wrong sleeves, then search everyone present over the course of the next three hours.

It turned out to have been a rival promoter who had phoned the cops and told them there was a bomb in the club.

MTV hosts The Cuban Brothers tell of getting lashed in a New Orleans strip joint and shimmying up the pole after the dancers. They only came down when, a few minutes later, four patrolmen stormed into the club, followed them up the pole, pistol-whipped them and hit them with a $4,500 fine.

It was a promoter contact of mine, rather than a DJ, who found himself in one of the tightest gig-related scrapes I've come across. I'd gone out to Vienna alongside the UK's DJ Swing,[4] to play for an ambitious 19-year-old Austrian promoter called David. Clearly influenced by hip hop videos, he'd sent a limo to pick us up from the airport, complete with in-car TV, champagne and a couple of reclining hip hop honeys to finish off the effect. Damn, we thought; this dude must be making some serious money!

It was more a case of borrowing some serious money. As a 19-year-old club promoter, your bank loan options are a little limited. David knew this, which is why he'd bypassed the banks altogether and gone to a loan shark instead. The loan shark was a pretty enterprising guy himself; he doubled as a prominent member of the Austrian mafia.

David made the classic mistake of blindly assuming he'd be able to repay all his debts by the proceeds from the gig. Unfortunately this wasn't the case. To his credit, he did pay Swing and myself in full, but we spent the following day

---

4. *R.I.P. to Swing, one of the best UK DJs to have ever done it.*

running all over Vienna before he dropped me back at the airport.

When we'd visited our third café in two hours, he told me what was happening. 'I can't stay in one place too long, or they might find me,' he explained. From what I gather, straight after dropping me off for my flight to London, David scraped together his remaining funds and leapt on one for Los Angeles. This guy was scared. He ended up staying for a year and meeting and marrying an American girl there in the process.

I thought I'd heard the last of him, but he popped back up in Austria a couple of years later. Maybe his shark had been wacked and the coast was clear. He re-booked me for a new gig, and this time I decided to take the girlfriend, so I booked an extra flight.

Reverting to true promoter type, David then cancelled the gig. Fair enough, I said, but you need to reimburse me for the extra flight now that we won't be coming. Unbelievably, David launched into a tirade about professionalism, and how it wasn't very businesslike for me to combine work with leisure by taking my girl on overseas trips. Tell me if I'm wrong, but I find it a little hard to swallow a lecture on professionalism from someone more than a decade my junior who borrows money from gangsters, doesn't pay it back, escapes to America for a year to avoid the results and indulges in a shotgun wedding while he's there!

But perhaps the biggest nightmare of all comes from my mate DJ D, the female turntablist from Australia. It reads like the hard-to-swallow plot to a farcical movie comedy, but D insists it's 100 per cent true. The story is best told by D herself, as she related it to the chat forum on my website:

"Last New Year's Eve, I'd been booked to play a big gig in the Middle East alongside DJ Solz. We knew the schedule involved 24 hours of travelling. What we didn't expect was the extra little surprises!

It started as soon as we hit check-in at the airport, where the attendant claimed we didn't have valid tickets to board. To try and resolve it, I had to make three calls to the Middle East on my mobile, at hideous expense.

Two hours later, she found the tickets sitting in an envelope right in front of her.

Next, it transpired that the airline had given us the wrong information about the baggage weight limits on the flight, and to get them to take all my records, I ended up having to pay over 600 dollars in excess charges. By the time this was sorted out, we were left with seconds to make the flight—the only one of the day.

Having boarded, it turned out we were seated behind the most unreasonable couple on the entire flight, who reclined all the way into our laps and refused to move. My personal TV didn't work. It smelled. We travelled like this for something like 20 hours.

We disembarked, only to find later that Solz had left his wallet and mobile on the plane, and I'd left a couple of good luck cards containing spending money on board. Next up was an eleven-hour stopover at the airport before we could continue travel.

A century or so later, we finally arrived at our designated airport, only to be stopped by the guards who spoke next to no English and fired a tirade of Arabic at us. We eventually made out "too much CD" as one of them pointed at Solz's records. We spent over five hours at the airport, tired, hungry, and with a gig to play that night.

After being patted down by a woman in a private room, the man in charge summoned me into his office. He began our conversation with 'I love Australian women'. 'Here we go," I thought.

Being New Year's Eve, all departments that could grant us entry were closed. We had two choices—leave our records behind and enter the country with nothing to play at our gig that night, or stay with the records and wait. Meanwhile, the promoter had already driven to both sides of the country twice to try and get authorisation.

Over five hours later, the promoter paid a substantial amount of money to get us into the country.

We were in. But the saga continued.

Next up, we were driven by a stranger, who once again did not speak English, to alternative accommodation which didn't match the initial agreement. It was 'unserviced', meaning no iron, no hairdryer, no room service, and a really loud 'clunk' sound as the air conditioning unit dripped straight on to another one right outside my window.

Later that day, we had a four-hour soundcheck, as the technicians didn't usually use turntables; they skipped and fed back constantly. We tried to conserve energy by lying on the floor at every possible chance.

We managed half an hour's sleep that day. Meanwhile, the poor promoter was doing everything he could to get us what we needed, but things just weren't happening. We finally went to the event with no food, no iron, no hairdryer.

Eventually, I started my set, and from that point on—mercifully—everything was just fine. All of that pain was definitely worth the roars that came from that crowd when I hopped up there, and the atmosphere was amazing. Something I'll never forget."

CHAPTER 18

DO US A TAPE

A DJ mix tape serves many functions. At the very least it can liven up a club manager's in-car entertainment.

As any musician will tell you, submitting a demo tape is a standard way of securing a gig. It's not much different in the DJing world. Unless you're Chris Moyles or Jo Whiley, it's the first thing you'll be asked for by a programme controller when trying to secure a radio slot. And in clubland, it's all about mix tapes,[1] an opportunity for a promoter or venue to get a feel for your musical style and creative approach before booking you.

Many find being asked for a 'demo tape' demeaning—particularly those who have been in the game for a while. It implies that your name and apparent status alone is not enough to merit a booking, and the promoter requires some tangible evidence that you can actually mix two tunes together, despite all your big talk. It's fair enough, I suppose.

---

1. *Another now-redundant throwback, but a Spotify playlist just doesn't have the same effect.*

The DJ game does tend to attract its share of chancers, and the decision-makers need some way of sorting the sheep from the goats. It's also sensible by way of establishing whether a particular DJ's style is right for the sound of a particular club.

I started producing mixtapes many moons ago, when they really were cassettes, and when the notion of actually being able to produce your own CDs[2] was still something you gazed at, open-mouthed, on 'Tomorrow's World'. The earliest form of these contained what I referred to as 'pause button mixes.' I was amused to hear the otherwise monumentally-unfunny Peter Kay touch on this in a sketch when he talked about taping the top 40 off the radio as a kid, and trying to hit the pause button before Tommy Vance started his back-announcement. You could never quite get it, of course.

In my version, long before I'd ever heard of DJ mixers and vari-speed turntables, I used to create my own 'MD remixes' of records I'd bought by recording key sections on to cassette, then attempting to edit in a new section by painstakingly releasing the pause button at precisely the right moment to catch the beat. Of course, I missed it nearly every time, so I'd go back and do it over and over again until I was satisfied with the result.

A variation on this was to try and re-create the so-called 'digital delay' effect that was all the rage in 1980s pop dance. This was achieved by recording a millisecond of vocal, then pausing the cassette, putting the needle back to the exact same spot, releasing the pause button again, and so on, maybe as many as fifteen times. Looking back now, I'm amazed I had the patience. It's fairly apparent I didn't have a girlfriend. I still have the resulting cassettes sitting under cobwebs and dust in the garage, but they're just too

---

2. *Already been and gone!*

painful to listen to. I can trace these to as far back as the age of thirteen.

The amazing thing is that some aspiring DJs actually submit tapes that are of no better overall quality than this when trying to secure gigs. I know this because I sat on the judging panel of the Fosters Ice DJ Academy during my time at Galaxy 101, and was obliged to listen to stacks of appalling entries for several weeks. One tried to beat-mix Bob Marley's 'One Love' into Kool And The Gang's 'Celebration'. Trust me, it can't be done.

Most DJs get the point, though, and put their all into anything they're going to try and use to stand out from their competitors and get themselves some work. It's satisfying when these impress the recipient and achieve the desired effect, but that's a rare occurrence.

In most cases, a follow-up call is inevitable, and the promoter will usually claim that he's not received it, and can you send another one? You get the impression half the time that they just fancy a hot new CD for the car, and don't want to shell out £12.99 at HMV for the latest 'R&B Anthems' instalment. One particular club manager made several such requests a few years ago. When I finally got an audience in his office, I saw a whole array of my volumes arranged neatly, in order, on the shelf behind him. He still hadn't booked me. At least I know where to go for a back-up archive.

Several more enterprising DJs I know have turned the mix CD act into a mini-industry, flogging them to local shops and hairdressers for in-store play, to the extent that the stores call them every so often anxiously requesting the next volume. Others have successfully managed to sell copies to their club managers as warm-up mixes to be played prior to their arrival. You've got to admire the front.

I once got one such request from a venue manager myself, who offered to buy a CD for that weekend. The problem was I really didn't have time to compile one, so shamefully, but enterprisingly, I presented him with a particularly slick mix done by one of my mates, and passed it off as my own. Well, I'm hardly the first DJ to have done this. Just make sure you can walk it like you talk it if a club actually goes ahead and books you!

All DJs love compiling tapes and CDs. It's part of the same conviction all DJs have that their musical taste and knowledge is far superior to that of the peasants around them. Even when not required to lay their tastes down to impress a potential employer, DJs are regularly compelled to put together their own selections anyway, and the most frequent inspiration for this is to try and impress a member of the opposite gender.[3]

It's a fairly safe bet that the vast majority of the world's DJs have done this at one point or another. I certainly have, on several embarrassing occasions. The first was at the age of sixteen, when trying to woo a girl who worked on the provisions section at Waitrose. It would be too damaging to my career to reveal some of the songs I put on there, but amazingly, they seemed to have the desired effect, as the girl reciprocated by compiling her own tape of songs that she said reminded her of me. I've never known whether or not to be flattered by the fact that this included The Carpenters and Debbie Gibson, though.

This compulsion still hasn't worn off. I compiled a valentines CD for my wife as recently as a couple of years ago. But I like to think the tune selection is rather more sophisticated than back then. Hopefully I am, too.[4]

---

3. *Who else remembers the days when there were still only two?!*

4. *Err, possibly not!*

CHAPTER 19

UPS AND DOWNS

*'Yeah, I just took an ecstasy.
Ain't no telling what the side effects could be.'*

Dr. Dre: 'Let's Get High' (1999)

*'I take a couple uppers,
I down a couple downers,
But nothing compares to these blue and yellow purple pills.
I been to mushroom mountain,
Once or twice but who's countin',
But nothing compares to these blue and yellow purple pills.'*

D12: 'Purple Pills' (2001)

*'Pick it, pack it, fire it up.
Come along,
And take a hit from the bong.
Put the blunt down, just for a second.
Don't get me wrong, it's not a new method.
Inhale, exhale...
Just got an ounce in the mail.'*

Cypress Hill: 'Hits From The Bong' (1993)

*'Either up your nose or in your vein,
With nothing to gain except killing your brain.'*

Grandmaster Melle Mel: 'White Lines' (1983)

Mark Devlin

The nightlife game is not without its narcotic temptations. Different DJs react in wildly differing ways.

In 2005, the British film 'It's All Gone Pete Tong' was released. Apart from marking the first time that a DJ's name has ever featured in a movie title, (it's modern rhyming slang for 'wrong', and has even earned itself a space in the English Dictionary as a result,) its plotline neatly sums up the way in which much of the outside world views the lifestyle of the average DJ.

The central role is that of DJ Frankie Wilde, (played by Dennis Pennis actor Paul Kaye,) and the film portrays his life through an Ibizan Summer as one long, narcotic-fuelled party, with everything in excess, from the booze and drugs to the sex to the pay packets

It's not actually the drugs that get him in the end; his constant exposure to ear-splitting music levels cause him to go deaf—not an ideal predicament for a DJ. For many, however, the drug-related aspects of Frankie's life will be considered pretty close to the mark.

Drug culture in the UK club scene passed the point of taboo many years ago. Most commentators agree that the turning point was 1987/ 88, the infamous era of the so-called Acid House and Balearic Beat movements. Their arrival coincided with the new fashionability of the drug ecstasy, or 'E', and it's pretty much been a part of mainstream dance music culture ever since.[1]

A big clue as to how far drug and dance culture had merged could be seen in nothing more complex than the

---

1. *All the products of a military-grade social-engineering operation—yet again, see 'Musical truth Volume 2'—little did I realise at the time.*

opening times of the big dance superclubs. As early as 1990, like the Northern soul clubs before them, most were staying open until 6 or 7 in the morning where licences allowed, and were still rammed at closing time. That much stamina from natural energy and dance-induced adrenaline? (The same suspicions may well arise from 'marathon' DJ sets that are frequently advertised. Junior Vasquez began one at New York's Tunnel club in 1995, for example, where he played non-stop from 11pm Saturday night to 2pm Sunday afternoon every week!)

E-culture became an accepted part of clubbing through the 90s, and nowhere was this more apparent than in the pages of the UK's most consistently popular dance music publication 'Mixmag', which aims at an average readership age of 18. Regular cover features with titles like...'Are Drugs Driving You Mad?' 'Jellies: The Mong-out Menace', 'Ecstasy: Scared?', 'Paranoid? You Should Be', '1993: Year Of The Trip', 'The Good Comedown Guide', and 'Taking The Piss: Drug Testing At Work' summed up the kind of lifestyle the magazine knew its readers were into, and through which it was able to connect meaningfully with them.

In November 1995, the party came to an abrupt stop. Teenager Leah Betts from Essex collapsed and died after necking a single ecstasy tablet at her 18th birthday party. The medical view was that the large amount of water she drank diluted her blood-sodium level to a dangerous extent, accentuating the effects of the pill. This was far from the first instance of death by E, but the government, police and local authorities instantly leapt on this one. The case was used to make an example of club-drug culture, initially involving a nationwide poster campaign featuring huge pictures of the teenager with the single slogan 'sorted' underneath.

Mark Devlin

The DJ world has had its occasional victim, too. Liverpool's Mark Johnson collapsed in January 1995, for instance, following a gig at the city's Voodoo club, and died shortly afterwards in hospital aged just 22. He had apparently taken an E.

Incredibly, in 1996 came the news that clubbers could now take out £100,000 worth of insurance against the risk of dying or being permanently disabled from taking ecstacy and other drugs, courtesy of a London firm, offering the deal for £15 a year—the price of an E!

In recognition of the extent to which E-consumption was inextricably linked to dance music clubbing—and therefore their profits—many venues were keen to be showing themselves as taking a responsible stand on the issue. They provided free drinking water to help prevent clubbers from dehydrating at one end of the scale, and put trained medics on hand to give professional help in the case of any incidents at the other. Further measures have included temperature-regulated dancefloors, ventilation, and 'chill-out zones'—relaxing areas of a club away from the mayhem of the main dancefloor.

Things have settled down a lot since those heady days, when the tabloid press seized any opportunity to run scaremongering stories on the 'evils' of drug use linked with clubbing. It's now such an integral part of the scene it's no longer considered news.

The urban music world has its different drugs of choice. Canabis has long been a favourite of the hip hop and reggae genre, and has earned itself at least twenty slang names in the lyrics of hip hop records alone![2]

The faster beats and tempos of drum and bass, UK garage and grime, meanwhile, may well have been fuelled partly by an enthusiasm towards cocaine and speed.

---

2. *How many can you name?!*

Whatever the case, music and drugs have been fundamentally linked for generations, and it hardly looks likely to change. As ever, it's down to any one individual as to what stance they're going to take on the situation.

Personally speaking, drugs have never figured majorly in my life, either before or after my DJing career took off. I tried weed a few times, largely in a young and foolish quest to gain acceptance and credibility in the circles I found myself moving in. It only took a few goes for me to realise that I wasn't really getting anything out of it.

It just used to make me feel drunk and giggle and talk crap a lot. (If it weren't for the fact that I gave up on trying to maintain it years ago, I'd be putting my reputation on the line by admitting that I actually passed out from it once. I will, however, quantify that by pointing out that it was in an Amsterdam coffee shop in the middle of an afternoon when I'd already put away a few beers, and it was a particularly potent blend, as tends to be the case in 'Dam...just in case you think I'm that much of a lightweight!)

Other than that, I was talked into trying speed once, and as far as I can make out, nothing happened. So besides alcohol, that's it.

For most of my DJ friends on the house/ dance music side of the fence, it's different. One has invited me to try a chemically fuelled weekend on a few occasions, but I've always resisted.

Many of his attempts occurred when I was already in my late 20s, and my reaction then was that it would be a bit dumb having gone all though my teenage years and early 20s as clean as a whistle, to finally succumb at the age of 28.

His argument was that, on the contrary, that's the ideal age to try it. Then, you're more mature and far more able to do things responsibly than if you were ten years younger. As a result, you're far more likely to get the best effect from the gear. He may have a point. But I've still held back.

If nothing else, it just seems to be unnecessary expenditure.

CHAPTER 20

THE GREAT GIG IN THE SKY

'Don't feel guilty if you don't know what you want to do with your life. The most interesting people I know didn't know at 22 what they wanted to do with their lives. Some of the most interesting 40-year-olds I know still don't.
'Don't worry about the future. Or worry, but know that worrying is about as effective as trying to solve an algebra equation by chewing bubblegum.'

Baz Luhrmann: 'Everybody's Free To Wear Sunscreen' (1999)

'I'm done for now, so one for now,
Possibly for ever. We had fun together.
But like all good things, we must come to an end.
Please show the same love to my friends.
Dear Summer.'

Jay-Z: 'Dear Summer' (2005)

One of the most perplexing things about being a DJ, is that you age, but your crowd never does. The scene keeps rejuvenating, throwing off ageing punters at one end of the scale, and replacing them with new, fresh-faced ones at the other.

An unfortunate spin-off of this is that, as clubbers get older and stop going out, they take their musical heritage with them...which means that the impact that the big tunes from that era generated is lost also.

It can be seen clearly. There are now very few hip hop or house records from prior to 1990 that could be dropped in the average High Street club to great reaction. Far from retaining a status as evergreen gems, most are likely to be considered crusty old relics, and most DJs playing them will be rewarded with a thinning dancefloor.

Interesting to think that the same fate lies in store for today's big hits by the time a new generation hits clubland and starts claiming its own modern anthems. (And tragic to think that the likes of Boyzone, Westlife, Hearsay, Steps, McFly, Busted and other cynically manufactured acts will be heralded in 20 years with the same nostalgia that 80s legends like The Human League, Adam And The Ants, Duran Duran and Altered Images now are! The current generation of pop fans have a right to feel cheated!)[1]

In Eminem's famous 'diss' record on Benzino, then-editor of the US hip hop magazine 'The Source', who attempted to turn rap artist a few years ago, he derides him with the line 'nobody wants to see their Grandfather rap!' (Benzino was Eminem's considerable senior.)

Fair point. And the same is true of DJs. Most clubbers will have experienced a past-sell-by-date jock behind the decks at some point, and it's not a happy sight. The US DJ Whoo Kid, Eminem's tour DJ, agrees. "80 per cent of the DJs in America are ugly, chubby and goofy," he told me when I interviewed him for the UK's Touch magazine. "Mostly bald. DJing is a way to get somewhere else. It's

---

1. *It was bad then! I had no idea how much lower things would sink!*

not good to be 50 years old, bald and fat and still DJing.[2] That's not where I plan to be!"

Quite apart from the embarrassment factor, you might find it difficult staying awake after midnight. The Horlicks beckons.

Despite this, however, a significant proportion of the world's top-league DJs are now well over 40[3]—Paul Oakenfold, Norman Cook, Pete Tong, Dave Pearce, Roger Sanchez, Dave Morales, Tim Westwood, Trevor Nelson, Fabio, Grooverider, Gilles Peterson. Danny Tenaglia, Frankie Knuckles, Grandmaster Flash, Kool Herc, (considered the DJ who invented hip hop,) and Afrikaa Bambaataa are closer to 50, and are still going strong.[4]

For this lot, having been at the top of the tree for so long makes their unwillingness to give it all up entirely understandable. That's why they're all clinging on to what they've got for as long as possible.

None of them have to worry too much from a career perspective, of course. When they finally hang up the headphones there'll be no shortage of options elsewhere in the music game—record label or music production jobs, behind-the-scenes executive or consultancy roles, running artist or DJ management companies. If all else fails, they can probably maintain a highly respectable living appearing on all those 'Top 100 Greatest...' TV shows for at least a few years!

Most of them already make music, so there's no end of options there; Oakenfold began scoring Hollywood movies

---

2. *One sympathises.*

3. *Try over 60 now!*

4. *We don't talk about Bambaataa any more. See 'Musical Truth Volume 2'!*

years ago, which should see him well for a good while yet. None of the above will have to worry too much about their financial futures, either. They could retire tomorrow and be made for life.

It's not a question of what else they could possibly do that keeps them hanging on. It's fear of losing the incredible infectious buzz that DJing brings. They're in no hurry to lose their grip on their long-standing exuberant lifestyles. A constant gripe of young wannabe DJs in the letters pages of the dance music press is that the oldies just refuse to budge and let the new generation in. But can you really blame them?

For female DJs, there are other issues, as highlighted by hard house spinner Lisa Lashes talking to the Skruff news website in 2005.

"I don't think there's a time that's going to be right to have a baby, because I'd have to take two years out.

"Would it be worth going back into DJing after a two-year break? Am I ready to finish right now? Do I want a child? Would I regret having a child if it meant I was forced to sacrifice my career? Will I be too old by that time? Will my fallopian tubes have seized up by then?! I've got no idea. Of course, they're all questions that I've thought about, but what can I do?"

Anyway, that's the superstars. What about the rest of us? What are the prospects for the hordes of regular everyday jocks when we finally concede that we're getting old enough to be the grandparents of many of the kids we see dancing before us, let alone the parents?

Given all the perils detailed in this book, you might ask yourself why on earth any of us continue at all, and why we don't just find ourselves jobs that are less risky, more financially stable, and more socially respectable.

We can't. Like the superstars, this is what we do. It's part of us, and nothing else is good enough. There are some very powerful motivating factors at work when it comes to DJs. While the odd exception might be in it for the money or the drugs or the girls, nine times out of ten it's all down to an unquenchable passion and enthusiasm for the music we play.

It doesn't matter what you play, either. Whether it's house, techno, drum and bass, hip hop, pop—even an across-the-board wedding selection, DJs do what they do because they love their music, and the biggest buzz on earth is to be able to play it to as many people as possible, and hope they get the same kind of excitement out of hearing it.

Being a DJ might not be the most important, profound or intellectually-demanding job in the world. But I like to think it does have its meaningful aspects—if it's done right. Where I see the DJ's job fitting into the grand scheme of things is in offering people some relief and entertainment from the stresses or the drudgery of their everyday lives

While to us, a DJ set is what we do for a living, to a punter, it's their passport to having a great night out. From that point of view, we have a responsibility and a role, in that it's down to us whether or not our crowd go home with a smile on their face and a tune ringing in their ear, feeling they've got their money's-worth.

And the world's a pretty scary and depressing place at the best of times,[5] as a random glance at any given newspaper constantly reminds us! So I think it's important to have people who specialise in entertainment, and giving people some relief from all the doom and gloom.

There's a world of difference between this kind of positive mental approach and that of a sloppy DJ who couldn't care less, and who takes the view that his punters

---

5. *What did I know?!*

are going to get what they're given and they can damn-well please themselves. Most people can't tell the difference between a good DJ and a bad one—until they hear a bad one play!

For the new generations of DJs yet to come, prospects are so much brighter than they were as little as 15 years ago. DJing is no longer frowned upon as a career path. If it's combined with the actual creation of music, it's now considered on a par with being a pop star in terms of glory.

And the pay—if you make it big—is about as good as you can expect from any job. It's almost certainly the best-rewarded profession that doesn't require a university degree, or any other form of education or formal training, for that matter.

Everyone has a theory on whether DJing can be taught, or whether it's simply in the blood, like being a master painter or a great violinist. I'd be inclined towards the latter. Although the mechanics of it can be imparted, you've either got the rhythm and the skill for it inside you or you haven't. If you have, it's something you'll know about!

*

In Midge Ure's[6] 2004 auto-biography, he talks of having lived an ordinary life, punctuated by the occasional extraordinary moment. That's pretty much how I see my ride through the DJ game so far—though on a far more low-key scale than anything Midge or anyone of his ilk has done, of course!

There have been days of drudge where I've felt like jacking it all in—I've been seriously close to it at least three times. Then, without warning, your fortunes reverse and you find yourself jetting off to some exotic spot you'd

---

6. *Freemason and Chosen One!*

probably never have visited if it weren't for your job, or meeting Dr. Dre[7], or simply being complimented on what you do by some fans, and it all reminds you why you decided to do this thing in the first place.

Yeah, retirement from this job is a hard thing to do. Former Radio 1 jock Danny Rampling put it well in his press statement announcing his bowing-out at the end of 2005[8] to become a restaurateur in London.

"Looking back from where I am today as a man, a husband and a father, I am humbled to have played a part in a time that will go down in humanity as a musical revolution. A time when music took a powerful seat at the table of world's change and made its impact globally to millions of happy people.

"Those 18 years on the DJ stage have been such a brilliant experience. Sharing music and love with people all around the world in the darkest corners to the most fabulous settings always spreading the true vibe of house music with its message of peace and harmony.

"During the forthcoming last few months I'm certain that some of the gigs leading up to my finale on New Years Eve will get emotional."

Rampling's move seems to have been inspirational. House don Erick Morillo has since announced his intention to bow out at the end of 2006.[9]

In my view, there are three good reasons for retiring from being a DJ, and they're factors any jock could do well to consider seriously at least once a year.

---

7. *I'll pass!*

8. *That didn't last long!*

9. *Morillo was accused of multiple counts of sexual abuse by many women prior to his sudden death in 2020.*

a. When you're getting bored, and you no longer get the same buzz as you did when you first started out.

b. When you're no longer relevant, and can no longer cut it with your crowds.

c. When you start looking too old and are, quite frankly, an embarrassment. (This is not an issue in nostalgia-fuelled revival nights like Northern soul and the like, but becomes one when the next oldest person in the building is twenty years your junior.)

I've addressed all of these myself this year, and I'm happy to say the answer has been negative on all counts! So I intend to keep going for a bit longer yet.

Yeah, on reflection, despite all the crazy stuff you've read, I still wouldn't change my job for anything, and can't imagine myself feeling truly fulfilled doing anything else.

...except perhaps writing another book?[10]

---

10. *Well, at least that one worked out!*

APPENDIX 1

A collection of miscellaneous and bizarre DJ-related stories, direct from the front line.

The high-flying dance DJs have enjoyed some incredibly mindblowing experiences in the course of their jobs. Dutchman Tiesto played at the 2004 Olympics, propelling him to global stardom in the process, (and followed it up with an '05 gig at Disneyland Paris—a bit of a step downwards in the circumstances!), while Paul Oakenfold has performed on the Great Wall Of China and at the Burning Man Festival in the Nevada desert, to name but two. No shortage of stories to tell the grand-kids there.

But the most privileged character of all is undoubtedly Carl Cox, whose New Year's Eve 1999 wasn't just a once-in-a-lifetime experience; it was the first time anyone had experienced it in human history, and couldn't again for a thousand years. He began by seeing in the new millennium on Bondi Beach in Sydney, Australia, before hopping on a private jet for a seven-hour spin back round the globe, through several time zones, effectively chasing the midnight hour in the process. He disembarked in Hawaii—one of the last countries to see in the new year, where he then played a second midnight set. Now that'll take some beating on New Year's Eve 2999. (Although by then, they'll probably be holding raves on the moon—no, seriously!)

As if winning top spot in DJ Magazine's coveted Top 100 DJs Poll, and the Olympics and Disneyland gigs weren't enough, Dutch trance DJ Tiesto cemented his true superstar status even further in 2005 by becoming the first DJ to inspire a waxwork model at Holland's Madam Tussauds. Naturally enough, the sculpture appears behind a turntable, with visitors invited to mix music 'in conjunction' with the effigy.

It's always satisfying to learn the big guns are prone to the same dumb errors as the rest of us. Radio 1's R&B guru Trevor Nelson drove all the way from London to the Southport Weekender in the North West not so long ago. After a journey of several hours, (because let's face it, Southport is faaaa-aaaar!), he was horrified to open his boot and find he'd left all his records at home. The next time he set off he took extra care and the records arrived...but he left his suitcase containing all his clothes at home instead.

The origins of DJing stretch back much farther than most people imagine. It all began in a hired hall above a working men's club in Otley, West Yorkshire. In the 1940s, licenced premises entertainment in the UK was all about big bands, orchestras and dances. The first character to break the mould by adopting the then-revolutionary idea of playing pre-recorded gramophone records in dancehalls was to become a household name as a result. He's still one today. It was Jimmy Savile.

All the talk of 'DJs' in this book may well confuse anyone involved in the Jamaican reggae dancehall scene. In that world, a 'DJ' is an MC, the host of a party who chats and 'toasts' over the tracks. The DJ is the 'selector'.

Tales from the Flipside

I'm often told my hectic overseas travel schedules border on the absurd. But nothing I've done comes close to rivalling Judge Jules, who once flew all the way from London to Brisbane, Australia, to perform just one gig. After only ten hours on Australian soil, he was straight back on the plane home again.

Does the DJ world have Elton John-like divas to rival anything the pop world has to offer? Judge for yourself. New York house DJ Junior Vasquez turned down an offer of £10,000 in 1994 to travel to London to play a night at Ministry of Sound. "I wouldn't go over there and play Ministry," he commented at the time. "It's just stupid. Everybody does that." He then seemed to relent, however, admitting he'd be interested in coming over to play four or five records, rather than a full set. "Cause they're going to have the same records, and I'd be flattered if they'd let me play an hour."

At the same time, Vasquez took the opportunity to apologise to UK DJ Sasha after an altercation in the DJ booth at the Sound Factory in New York, where Vasquez held the residency. "I know that he felt I was kind of being rude to him," he commented. "I'm very close to this place, and I just can't bear to see other DJs play this room."

Vasquez eventually played outside the US and Canada for the first time ever when he hit Japan the following year, for a reported fee of $150,000.

(Mixmag, December 1994 and October 1996)

De La Soul once said 'everybody wants to be a DJ', and it seems it's as true of struggling celebs as much as the general public. In 1995, Home nightclub in Manchester operated its Foundation night, which offered celebrities the chance to step up to the decks and try and impress the crowd with a quick turn. New Order's Bernard Sumner, Liam Gallagher, Johnny Marr, Craig Gill and Martin Walsh of indie group The Inspiral Carpets, Nigel Pavarro, better known as Terry Duckworth from Coronation Street, and Ryan Gigs were among the early contenders. According to the club, Bernard Sumner wasn't bad at all.

Occasionally, crowd situations can get ugly in the club. Just ask poor old DJ 279, hip hop DJ and promoter of the infamous ill-fated Busta Rhymes concert at The Forum in Kentish Town, London in 1996. After Busta failed to show, seemingly over a complication with his work permit, 279 took on the grim task of addressing the throng of ticket-holders. The news didn't go down too well, sparking a riot, and causing one disgruntled punter to leap on stage, wrench one of the DJ's turntables free from its wiring, and run out into the street with it. He was last seen in Camden Town, still clutching the deck.

New Zealand's customs officials are notorious for their hard-edged stance on drugs, and as a result, visiting DJs tend to be subject to rigorous questioning and search procedures. Just ask UK hard house DJ Lisa Lashes. She was caught with two ecstasy tablets in her record bag when she visited in 2000. She claimed they were a plant, and must have been put there by a fan 'trying to be nice.' She was relatively lucky, getting away with several hours in custody, and fines of 100 New Zealand Dollars. If the pills had been found in Malaysia, her port of call prior to NZ, she would have faced the death penalty!

Along similar lines, Sandy Rivera, head honcho of the US house label Defected, was frequently finding himself in custody at various immigration offices in the UK and Europe not so long ago. His passport was seemingly arousing suspicion, and on one occasion, he was escorted to a plane for instant deportation. It was later found out that all he was really wanted for was some minor traffic offences and unpaid parking fines, and the problems were due to a glitch in the immigration system.

According to Mixmag in June 2004, a fan who had put a jar to UK superstar DJ Sasha's arse and bottled one of his farts managed to sell it on eBay for 99p. True, or a load of hot air? You decide.

It could be said that Tim Westwood, universally regarded as Europe's most successful and influential hip hop DJ, has paid a high enough price for his status. Following years of beatings outside club spots, (including one at an open-air pool party,) plus being stabbed and contracting an infected leg after an unpleasant diving accident in Jamaica, the ultimate ordeal came in July 1999 when he was shot in a drive-by attack after playing in Brockwell Park, South London. Having taken a bullet in the leg, Westwood shrugged off the attack, observing 'what doesn't kill you only makes you stronger'. He apparently kept the bullet as a souvenir.

Apart from Westwood at the time of his shooting, Norman Cook, aka Fatboy Slim, is the only other DJ to have regularly graced the pages of the UK tabloid press, largely as a result of marrying TV personality Zoe Ball. Things reached fever pitch in early 2003 when the pair announced a temporary trial separation following Zoe's affair with Z-list musician Dan Peppe. Not only was his Hove beachfront house immediately besieged by paparazzi, Norm later discovered his phone had been tapped in an attempt to obtain some dirt—surely the only time this has ever happened to a DJ?!

One of the most revered DJs in the 1970s/ 80s soul/ funk scene of the South East, and unofficial frontman for the so-called Soul Mafia movement, was Chris Hill. It's the same Chris Hill that went on to have a novelty Christmas pop hit in 1975 with 'Rent A Santa'. But Chris probably prefers to forget that these days.

Energy and charisma certainly goes far in a DJ performance. This was amply demonstrated by former Boogie Bunch member and MOBO Award winner DJ Swing when I played alongside him in Vienna in 2000. A short while into his set, Swing stopped the music altogether, stepped out from the decks, and went on to perform an impromptu comedy set for a full twenty minutes. He held the crowd's attention throughout—all the more impressive considering half of them didn't speak English—before going back to the music. It's hard to imagine any other DJ getting away with this. Tragically, Swing died from multiple myeloma, a form of skin cancer, in March 2006, a very great loss to the profession.

1987 marked the height of the 'rare groove' era, a movement largely sparked by Kiss FM London DJ Norman Jay, who was known for digging out rare and forgotten soul and funk gems from the archives and giving them a new lease of life. This led to a bout of snobbishness from many other DJs who tried to out-do him by unearthing ever more obscure nuggets. The practice drew contempt from Pete Waterman of the Stock Aitken Waterman crew. To highlight the pretentiousness, they produced 'Roadblock', which went on to become a chart hit. The early copies appeared on white label, however, and the track was cunningly passed off as an authentic early 70s rarity. Many 'cool' DJs fell for the trick, only to be horrified to later discover it had come from the crew behind Bananarama and Rick Astley. Most DJs deny being caught out, but hats off to my fellow Blues & Soul magazine colleague Pete Haigh for being brave enough to admit it!

Longevity is one of Pete's strengths. He's presented his 'On The Wire' show continually on BBC Radio Lancashire since 1984—surely some kind of record? Other impressive feats include the late James Hamilton's unbroken reign of providing his highly influential dance music column for 'Record Mirror', and later 'Music Week', every week from 1975 to his death in 1996, and Bob Jeffries, Billy Davidson, Bob Jones and Simon Mansell, the only DJs to have performed at every single one of the bi-annual Southport Weekenders since their inception in 1987.

It's a big deal for a DJ to be termed a 'pioneer', but in the case of Greg Wilson, there are few who'd disagree. He was one of only a handful of DJs to leap on the New York-style electro hip hop sound of the very early 80s and introduce it to clubbers in the North. As well as some spot-on mixing of groundbreaking new sounds on turntables, one of his tracks also involved mixing in the more hard-to-find stuff off of reel-to-reel tape machines. Having attempted this myself, I can testify that it's quite a feat!

The problems that illegal downloading of tracks causes to the music industry are well-documented. In early 2005, the DJ world received a wake-up call when an Italian jock was fined £1.4 million Euros, (almost £1 million,) for playing illegally-downloaded MP3s in his DJ sets. He was apparently found to be in possession of more than 2,000 'illegal' MP3s when police raided his gig in Rieti, near Rome. The heavy-handed fine is the biggest of its kind, and was designed to make an example of the DJ in question as a method of deterring others.

APPENDIX 2

MUSIC IS THE ANSWER

Nothing conjures up nostalgic memories as powerfully as music, and one of the greatest privileges of a DJ is being associated with playing the tunes that have that effect.

The following is a list of DJs and the tracks they played which have stayed with me the most. Whenever I hear each tune now, I remember it was these jocks who first brought it into my life. Doubtless everyone reading this book could compile their own list of this kind.

(In many cases, there are far more tracks that I could least for each DJ, but in the interests of brevity, I'm limiting things to five tracks each. Pete Tong and Tim Westwood are exceptions as they've both had two distinct radio stints, so they're allowed a section for each. It's my list, so I can do this!)

Radio:

ROBBIE VINCENT
(Radio 1. 1984—1987)

Shirley Murdock: As We Lay
Vision: The Seduction
Raze: Jack The Groove

Lola: Wax The Van
Chanelle: One Man

JEFF YOUNG
(Radio 1. 1987-90)

M.A.R.R.S: Pump Up The Volume
D-Mob: We Call It Acieeed
Ten City: That's The Way Love Is
Sterling Void: Runaway Girl
Lil' Louis: French Kiss

PETE TONG
(Capital Radio. 1987-90)

Mariah Carey: Vision Of Love
Diana Brown & Barry K Sharpe: The Masterplan
Fatman & Stella Mae: Release Me
Bobby Konders: The Poem
Happy Mondays: Step Off (Oakenfold Remix)

TIM WESTWOOD
(Capital Radio. 1987-94)

LL Cool J: Mama Said Knock You Out
Pete Rock & CL Smooth: They Reminisce Over You
Snoop Doggy Dogg: Doggy Style (the entire album!)
Nas: It Ain't Hard To Tell
Notorious BIG: Juicy

PETE TONG
(Radio 1. 1991- present)

Sharon Forrester: Love Inside
Goldie: Inner City Life
Dawn Penn: You Don't Love Me (No No No)
Roy Davis Jr: Gabriel

Mark Devlin

Shapeshifters: Lola's Theme

TIM WESTWOOD
(Radio 1. 1994—present)

Mobb Deep: The Shook Ones, Part 1
2Pac: Hit 'Em Up
Notorious BIG: Who Shot Ya
Foxy Brown: Get Me Home
Lil Jon & The Eastside Boys: Get Low

TREVOR NELSON
(On Radio 1. 1996- present)

Changing Faces: Stroke You Up
Erykah Badu: On & On
Bobby Digital: Love Jones
Jill Scott: Getting In The Way
Bobby Valentino: Tell Me

DANNY RAMPLING
(On Radio 1. 1994-2001)

Lady Saw: Sycamore Tree
Wayne Wonder: Bashment Girl
Harlem Hustlers: Get On Down
The Face: Needin' U
Todd Terry: I'll Take You There

(To quantify the first two tracks, which are serious reggae tunes, Danny used to run a feature called 'The Easy Funky Three' which saw him deviate from his usual dance music format to cover other unexpected styles. Exactly what an open-minded creative DJ should do!)

Clubs:

GRAHAM GOLD
(At The Park End Club, Oxford. 1993)

Urban Cookie Collective: The Key, The Secret
Mariah Carey; Dream Lover (Morales Remix)
Alex Party: Read My Lips
Ideal: Hot
Screen II: Hey Mr. DJ

FUNKMASTER FLEX
(At The Tunnel, New York City. 1994-96)

Akafella: Put It In Your Mouth
Method Man & Mary J Blige: All I Need
Channel Live: Mad Izm
Ol' Dirty Bastard: Brooklyn Zoo
Heather B: All Glocks Down

DJ PREMIER
(At The Astoria, London. 2003)

Group Home: Superstar
Gang Starr: Full Clip
Nas: Nas Is Like
Capone N Noreaga: Invincible
Jeru Tha Damaja: Come Clean

DJ JAZZY JEFF
(At The Fez Club, Reading. 2005)

Deee-Lite: Groove Is In The Heart
Eurythmics: Sweet Dreams
Queen: Another One Bites The Dust
DJ Jazzy Jeff & The Fresh Prince: Summertime
Biz Markie: Nobody Beats The Bizz

One-offs:

MARK TONDERAI
(On Radio 1. 1993)

Souls Of Mischief: '93 To Infinity

CHRIS PHILLIPS
(At Notting Hill Carnival, London. 1994)

Lady Of Rage: Afro Puffs

DAVID RODIGAN
(At Matrix, Reading. 2002)

Tenor Saw: Ring The Alarm

KOOL DJ RED ALERT
(At Webster Hall, New York City. 2003)

Joe Budden: Pump It Up

THE RANKIN' MISS P
(Radio 1. Mid 80s)

Sister Nancy: Bam Bam

MATT WHITE
(At Hanover Grand, London. 1999)

Kelly Price & Aaron Hall: Love Sets You Free

CRUCIAL ROBBIE
(At The Penthouse, Hitchin. 2001)

T.O.K: Chi Chi Man

LEKAN
(At Blue Mountain Club, Bristol. 1997)

Busta Rhymes & Rampage: Flipmode Is The Squad

STRETCH TAYLOR
(At Club M, Newmarket. 2003)

Joe Budden: Fire (Yes Yes Y'all)

STEVE WREN
(At The Southport Weekender. 1998)

Horace Brown: Things We Do For Love

DJ SWING
(At Mautners, Vienna. 2000)

Aaliyah: Try Again

APPENDIX 3

CHAT FORUM—THE BEST BITS

A regular feature of my website from 2004 was the chat forum, where I started discussions on a range of topics and fellow DJs and other followers would chip in with their thoughts and opinions.

Here are a selection of the most popular threads. (Though the OCD grammar freak in me feels compelled to do otherwise, I have left the entries just as they appeared at the time, warts and all!)

THE DEATH OF VINYL??

Mark

Dance DJs now boast about how they can play their entire sets of CD, and the flexibility that the new generation of DJ CD mixers now offers them? Should hip hop/ R&B DJs be going the same way, or can their skills only really be achieved with vinyl? Is it possible for a real urban music DJ to be taken seriously if playing their entire set off CD? DJ or non-DJ—have your say!

Tales from the Flipside

DJ Geespot
(Port Elizabeth, South Africa)

Well I don't think urban music should be showcased on CDs.I know there are scratch cd players out there but they don't do it for me..I saw an advert on the honey movie but I believe if u wanna be the next grand master whatever one should stick to the old simple rules.Technology does evolve but I wont recognise someone playing CDs.

And i think it boils down to prices coz a vinyl single has the price tag of a full album on cd...So thats why DJs wanna go the CDs route..Now mi problem with em CDs is a lot of the collection that a DJ will have will be pirated copies.But with vinyls the artist is sure to gain from DJs. So lets promote this artists the vinyl way...

Mark

Well, I'm bound to be biased, cos when I started out DJing, vinyl was pretty much the only format that anyone used, and I've stuck with it throughout.

Certainly, the latest generation of CD mixers make it possible for DJs to perform all kinds of tricks that replicate vinyl—but how much of them are down to the creativity of DJ, rather than the versatility of the equipment. It's being made easier for even the sloppiest of DJs to sound half decent, purely down to the equipment they're spinning on!

Good old-fashioned vinyl still requires real skills, and encourages real creativity. I mean, can you see Jazzy Jeff, Cash Money or The Scratch Perverts doing a show off CDs? They'd be thrown off-stage!

Belfast's Finest
(Belfast, Northern Ireland)

This is a hot topic and no mistake. I can't make the transition from vinyl to CD—personally, I would be a bit of a luddite, my interest in technology stopped with the mobile phone, 'cause they're a pain in the arse...

But, yes, CD's are not your ideal tool for the urban DJ. I would rely on double copies of records for instrumentals and accapellas, these just aren't available on a bootlegged CD. I would also work off 3 decks on occasion—what need would I have for CD?

D-NO
(Newcastle, England)

I personal favour vinyl, as will most DJs I presume.

However, I stand by my CD-Js for practicality and their creative potential.

I believe CD-Js (unlike awful button-presser Denon CD Decks, etc) are the next best thing to a pair of 1210s and would have no problem doing a whole set from them if the need be.

In terms of practicality, they are ideal as you can manipulate a CD just as you can with vinyl (and more) without worrying about needle's skipping.

Also, for DJs that travel.. you might know what it's like to get stung with an excess baggage fee (try getting the promoter to cover that one!!!) usually costing around the same price as your flight (I got an 800 quid slap in the face from KLM Airways when I recently took my records to Dubai).

You can fit what you would put into 4 record bags onto about 40 CDs in one wallet.

Top DJs like Kofi have performed entire sets on CD-Js to fantastic effect. Check out my boy Devon, a DJ from Newcastle, ripping up a James Brown double with 2 CD-Js—Click Here

However, as said, I do favour vinyl for my sets and only venture onto CD to play my own remixes or new stuff that I haven't been able to get on wax yet.

Mark

True. The weight problem at flight check-ins is enough to justify a switch to CDs in itself! Fortunately, I've always managed to avoid excess weight fees by skilfully distributing my records between hold and hand luggage, (and in some cases hiding the odd bag at check-in. Ridiculous, but necessary!)

It would be sheer luxury to waltz on to a flight with all your tunes for that night's performance on one handy, light wallet. I can only dream.

The problem is, for a jock like myself, even if I did decide to make the switch to CD, it would take literally years to replace the massive vinyl collection I have on CD—or probably just as long to burn them off at home!

D-NO

Mark wrote:
Fortunately, I've always managed to avoid excess weight fees by skilfully distributing my records between hold and hand luggage...

...Or blaggi'n club class from the promoter more like!!!
Seriously though...KLM are really bad for this...
Others like China airlines will let you through even up to 30 kilos over.

Damn them dutch mans...

Mark

Nah man, Ryanair have to be the worst airline in the world. They're liars, and they truly, honestly don't give a shit. If anything goes wrong on a Ryanair flight, may God be with you, cos Ryanair won't!

I only fly with them when there's absolutely no alternative. I suggest everyone else does the same.

Mark

An interesting comment which arose this week. While talking to the manager of a big commercial nightclub about a forthcoming gig, the guy asked if I used CD or vinyl. When I said vinyl, he replied, 'oh, you're a proper DJ then! We had Judge Jules the other week, and he played totally off CD. It just looked like he wasn't doing anything at all!'

As I say, just an interesting outsiders' viewpoint to add some fuel to the fire.

DJ Geespot

Speaking of CD-Js I just thought about the whole business of how easy it is to make a loop on a CD-J at the press of a button while using vinyls u need 2 copies,and be a lil faster as u need to juggle between the 2 vinyls...Now where is art being shown,CD-Js or turntables .But anyway as for other music genres like dance music you don't need to use vinyls but as for hip hop I cant imagine The Allies,Mark Devlin or Xcecutioners doing their thang off CD.

Mark

Let's not front, DJing off CDs does require skill, and there's a whole new load of tricks you can learn over and above playing off vinyl. But it's all down to genres. Creating loops, samples, etc, may be all very good for house/ dance music, with its emphasis on long, dramatic mixes, and musical 'journeys', but how relevant are they to the hip hop style? Not really at all, I'd say. And show me any hip hop DJ who'd disagree!

D-NO

DJ Geespot wrote:

Speaking of CD-Js I just thought about the whole business of how easy it is to make a loop on a CD-J at the press of a button while using vinyls u need 2 copies,and be a lil faster as u need to juggle between the 2 vinyls...Now where is art being shown,CD-Js or turntables .

Yeah you could juggle by using loops but you can also emulate an old fashioned vinyl beat juggle on CDJs as the video clip with Devon demonstrates. I've also watched Kofi do some unbelievable shit on CDJs.

Also check out this demonstration clip from Pioneer: http://www.djsounds.com/videos/cdj-1000_broad.asx

The guy in the vid is'nt the best scratch DJ but it shows people who haven't used the CD-J how versatile it can be.

DJ Geespot

Well I never said you don't need skill to play CD-Js,but what I say I'll recognise someone playing vinyl more than someone playing CDs, especially when it comes to hip hop. Other genres I'm not worried that much and mi very first argument was.

Quote:

And i think it boils down to prices coz a vinyl single has the price tag of a full album on cd...So thats why DJs wanna go the CDs route..

Mark Devlin

And if i can steal a line from mark
Quote:
Certainly, the latest generation of CD mixers make it possible for DJs to perform all kinds of tricks that replicate vinyl—but how much of them are down to the creativity of DJ, rather than the versatility of the equipment. Good old-fashioned vinyl still requires real skills, and encourages real creativity.

Yeah you can do juggles without using the loops on CD-Js but I think u'll be wasting the brains of the person who made that loop button,let alone your time to learn new things u can do on the cd player(Just like Kofi,right D-NO).Well, I couldn't see the demo yet but I'll try and watch it. So I know u need skill to generate some tricks on the CD-Js but I'll always like a disk jockey who is using vinyls more than the one using CDs.(Especially hip hop DJs)

Mark

Personally, I would actually like to learn some of the tricks that can be performed on the new generation of CD mixers. I learned to mix on turntables 14 years ago, so a new set of skills would be a useful thing.

Someone just needs to create an eighth day of the week in order for me to get the time!

Mark

A DJ called Steve Sadler was playing before me at NYT in London on Friday. His set was tight, and it was only when I stepped into the DJ booth that I realised he'd been playing the whole thing off CD. Even I couldn't tell the difference.

Food for thought, anyway.

Tales from the Flipside

*

THE DEATH OF VINYL??

DJ Geespot

Yeah D-NO I have checked that video demo, and well its wack CD players. They are good coz they are made to be like turntables. I have seen some scratch CDJs before but those ones are on their own class. Coz u can even have over 3 cues on a song and search for a certain part through a track in seconds. They are great CDJs but still I'm saying f*%@ digital, vinyls is the way to go.

DJ D

It seems like the consensus is to go vinyl. This is truly my choice being a turntablist, and when I play this is what I use. None of this jumping back and forth between cd to vinyl, I stick to it, juggle it, scratch it, use body tricks, and love it not only for its rich warm sound, but for its feel and even its show factor. I mean what is more interesting, watching someone spin vinyl or watching someone push buttons? Try it sometime, its interesting how much more natural spinning vinyl looks...

Although this is my number one choice, i do own a pair of CDJs and have a friends DN S5000 with which i can scratch, and even beat mix tracks off the one cd, using just one deck. It's not the same as vinyl, but its a skill that I can add to my repertoire to use as a backup should something go wrong and for some reason I don't have access to a pair of decks.

It also depends on the types of gigs your playing, they can be handy for those chilled out all day events, when you have to be doing something else for ten minutes (like setting up the stage for performers) where you can whack on a cd and go do your thing.

In the club / concert scene however, I still drag my boxes of vinyl weighing over 50kilos, to play short sets. Hey, for a girl that ain't easy especially when there are flights of stairs involved.

So for safety & health reasons (as DJ Anush can vouch for now using final scratch at many of his gigs) it is much more convenient and easier to use. It's also a heck of a lot cheaper to download or burn tracks, than search for years to find them on vinyl.

But for me cd mixing lacks that 'old skool' feel. I love my vinyl. Nothing, no matter how good this technology gets (and the DN S5000 is pretty good), it will just never be the same. The whole digital sound lacks warmth and looks so mechanical. It just doesn't have that flow that you need to work with vinyl well.

Mark

Good point about the 'theatrical' aspect of DJing off vinyl. For years, the DMC/ Technics Mixing Championships have been built around this element—scratching with snooker cues, kitchen sinks, elbows, chins, etc. And remember DJ David's infamous turntable handstand? Just how exciting can watching someone press a few buttons be??

**DJ D
(Sydney, Australia)**

Hypothetically, if we were to see an increase in future 'CD DJs', this could work as a plus for us existing vinyl addicts.

It will retain a niche, making what we do somewhat 'rare' and 'special'. In this case vinyl could never die.

Mark

Yeah, I reckon no matter which way new technology goes, DJs will always keep the market for vinyl alive. How many non-DJ consumers out there do you think would buy an album on vinyl to listen to at home in preference to a CD? None! So, we DJs have been keeping the market for vinyl going for years already. And we'll continue to do so!

Jayzon
(Stockholm, Sweden)

I'm doing my first all CD-gig this Thursday, on Numark CDX's (which is as close to vinyl you can get, there's actually a real piece of vinyl attached for controlling the sound!).
  My feelings before this event:
  *Not having to worry about skipping needles
  *My back will aaaaaaiiiiiight the day after ...
  *Even though I'm bringing 10x more music than I usually do
  *Not having to be so selective before the gig (3 crates is usually my maximum).
  What do I do if a player breaks down on me??? (1200's are reliable)
  Having to flip through all of these small sleeves n stuff, recognizing 12"s in a crate must be easier
  Ripping the new 12"s into the CPU and burning them on CD's isn't really what I consider fun
  I'll just wait and see what the Digital Devil can offer me ...

Mark

I played a CD-only gig in Scotland last year, and hated it—although it was on conventional CD players, rather than DJ-friendly ones. As Jayzon says, the main problem is identifying the tracks in their sleeves. With vinyl, you can find a tune in a flash.
  Let us know ho the CD gig goes!

DJ D

Jay, what about cd's that skip? (i.e. surface scratch or dust)
  things that have happened to me when I used to play cd:
  *accidentality hitting the eject button
  *cd jammed in the console leaving one deck available
  *reaching over for my vinyl whilst setting up (another DJ playing cd) and accidentality hitting the stop button with my breast! lol. Quick recovery hitting play again, but it all happened whilst playing the naughty by nature after party
  Hope yours runs a lot smoother than that, good luck with it

Mark

Well, he doesn't need to worry about point no. 3!
  Just an aside on the subject of accidentally hitting the CD stop button, has anyone else ever accidentally hit the stop button on the wrong turntable before, ie the one that's playing? Or is it just me?!

D-NO

Never hit the wrong deck's stop button but I have accidentally hit the power on/off switch on a technics deck whilst scratching.

On Q-bert's DIY Scratching video theres a section called DJ tips which has a little tip in to combat this whereby you take the rubber ring from the arm and put it around the power switch to stop it being accidentally turned off.

Karl Cross
(Ipswich, England)

I prefer vinyl definitely, the flexibility and hands on is so much better and in my opinion no cd deck can rival it, and I've used loads, pioneer, Denon, Numark. (altho the loop thing on many cd's is fun!)

Plus 99.9% of my promos are wax. Problems i think, lie in many venues not supporting vinyl and only installing cd decks. usually because of space behind the DJ console, or unable to build a stable enough console to prevent stylus jumps and feedback. In one of my residencies I have access to both cd & vinyl altho you will see me use mostly cd as the decks are a jumpin' nightmare.

This means I then have to convert my new vinyl to cd, (is this legal or not?) Technically I still have the vinyl they are taken from, but thats another thread.

My Biggest hate is this new PC DJ sh##. Whats that about? Its so lazy, it BPMs beat matches and even finds the tracks for you. It takes all the fun out of mixing and looking for the track before the other one finishes. I'm sure these so called "DJ's" are shooting themselves in the foot, how long before the computer mixes itself and starts making customer announcements?

Peace, 3 Times at Least.
KC

Mark

Good point. It surely can't be long before certain venues cotton on to the idea of saving themselves a DJ wage bill, and just get an engineer to set one of these things up for the night.

Lee Drummond
(Bedford, England)

Having used both vinyl and CDs on their respective elements of technology, I still feel that we will not lose the elements of vinyl. The history is living and breathing in that piece of plastic that separates the die hard professionals from the new breed. The skills of the MIX is portrayed from the mind to the hand...digital technology depletes the need to think...it does it for you...watch out all you digital freaks ..the clubs will soon be programming their own CD mixers and will not need you lot anymore.

But listen to the sound.. why has digital technology not been able to emulate the real sound of the base on their tracks?? Vinyl always sounds beefier, rounder...digital may be louder...but thats as far as it goes with sound quality...and CDs do jump, hop and skip...at least with vinyl you can apply a little pressure to the needle and get away with it. The turntable rules...

DJ D

I have to share an experience with you.

When I played in Cairns last yr with DJ Dexta, I went to the ONLY rnb club in the area after the gig. Noticed the music wasn't being properly beatmx but had a boogie anyways whilst watching the video tracks. Got thirsty so I went to buy a drink, but when trying to give the bar tender some cash, he ran off. Confused, I turned around to see what had happened, only to notice & laugh that he was the DJ as well lol.. Just thought that was a good eg of computer technology taking over, & bar owners trying to cut costs..

What r peoples thoughts about using final scratch in the clubs?

DJ Geespot

I hate the idea of people using final scratch in clubs. But anyway because now its being promoted by prominent DJs like craze I think it'll get its way into many booths

THE DEATH OF VINYL??

DJ D

Yeah I kinda agree with you Geespot. I have had a little play with it, but am still sticking to my old skool vinyl techniques. I love searching for it, and buying big wads of it.. none of this downloading mp3s & all...

Mark

Damn! This subject has turned out to be the most popular on the site so far! I feel we should now immortalise it and lay it to rest—unless anyone has any final comments to make on the subject?

Thanks for all the interest and heartfelt comments so far!

Mark Devlin

DJ Geespot

A stone on the grave. I prefer vinyl to CDs. Period. Let me to other topics.

Mark

Have to say, the more spots I travel around to, the more I'm seeing DJs constructing entire sets off CD—these are hip hop DJs, too.
 So you never know... it could happen!

**Chippie
(London, England)**

Yeah loads of DJs are on the CD tip.. I dunno though, I 'm a real vinyl fan, it was one of the reasons I started DJing. Just knowing the control is in your hands is great... I even sold most of my CDs when I first started buying records... maybe that wasn't a good move...?

Mark

Well, you can always burn all your vinyl tracks on to CD if you ever decide to go down that route. It's a little more difficult the other way round!

**DJ Hix
(Belfast, Northern Ireland)**

I know i'm a bit late on this one, but i think Final Scratch is a fantastic way of using vinyl without breaking your back carrying records everywhere.
 I saw Jazzy Jeff using it a few months back, and it was tremendous. i'd use final scratch before i would go all-cd.

DJ D

If I absolutely had to I would also use final scratch before I went cd..

However if I had a choice its vinyl all the way..

Come on fellas, if a girl of my size can carry around heavy crates, I'm sure you fellas can do it too! it ain't so bad...

Mark

I've just accrued an entire chapter for my forthcoming book!

Mark

I'd fully expected to lay this topic to rest, but can't do it without adding a footnote to last night's Jazzy Jeff DJ show, which I caught in Reading.

This was totally spellbinding! Jeff amazed the crowd by putting in a two-hour set entirely off of Final Scratch. So he was still manipulating the turntables in the same way as an old-school vinyl DJ would, but all the music was held on a small Apple Mac laptop, avoiding the need to keep slapping new records down on the turntables, and lug heavy crates into the club. He absolutely ripped through breaks, changing tune on average around every 30-45 seconds.

A true master at work, and a shining example of what can be achieved with new technology while still retaining old skills and techniques.

**UK VIP Pimp
(London, England)**

A DJ called Steve Sadler was playing before me at NYT in London on Friday. His set was tight, and it was only when I stepped into the DJ booth that I realised he'd been playing the whole thing off CD. Even I couldn't tell the difference.

Food for thought, anyway.

the only food that cd's will be giving is food for the license peeps when they come & check your collection ...

Mark

Along similarly-related lines, Numark are apparently in the latter stages of developing a new iPod mixer. Two Pods can connect directly into the mixer via the dock connections. MP3s can then be cued up and mixed.

Just wait for the automatic pilot function and DJs can consider themselves redundant!

D-NO

Lots of big name DJs are using Serato now including the likes of Jazzy Jeff and Clinton Sparks.

The CD argument is wearing a bit thin and the medium is being stereotyped with comments like that above. Not every CD is a bootleg copy and I bet the 'wax only luddites' wouldn't think twice about using a white label bootleg vinyl (for which no PRS royalties would have been paid to the artist).

I use both media as they both have distinct advantages and will shortly be using Serato as I've heard nothing but first hand praise for the product.

New technologies should be embraced and used as a platform to better oneself.

*

DANCE MUSIC AND URBAN MUSIC

The gulf widens. Why are the dance dudes so far ahead?

Mark

Why is the dance music world miles ahead of the urban music scene in so many aspects of the game? Although hip hop and R&B is now a global movement in the way house/dance music achieved a few years before, there's still a huge gulf between the two scenes in many areas. And it's more notable on DJing side of the game than anywhere:

* Dance DJs get paid vastly superior sums to their R&B counterparts, and enjoy a luxury lifestyle courtesy of clubs and promoters that book them—limos, private jets, penthouse suites, etc. An alien world to the average R&B jock.

* The house music world has spawned armies of household name DJs. Who in the UK hasn't heard of Fatboy Slim, Paul Oakenfold, Judge Jules, Pete Tong, Carl Cox, Danny Rampling, Sasha, etc. The urban world can only compete with Westwood, Nelson and Spoony... then you start to get stuck! Why do urban DJs not make it to household name status?

* Dance music events are staged on a much larger scale than urban events—sports stadiums, outdoor festivals, etc. They make shedloads more money. They also run much more smoothly, are rarely cancelled, and are seldom shut down by police or local authorities—unlike urban!

* You rarely get fights or idiots pulling guns/ knives in a house music
event...unlike urban!
* The dance music world has spawned 'superclub' brands like Cream, Gatecrasher, Slinky, Golden, etc, all with their own tag-on merchandising, representing major market-force brands as a result. OK, the urban world can offer Smoove and Twice As Nice, but again, that's where it stops.
...it goes on. Anyway—over to you!

**Sam Young,
(London, England)**

The gulf between the two isn't that big. In a lot of the London clubs I play at, they like to hear R&B, hip hop and funky house all in one night. I love playing all three, so it's a pleasure for me to see crowds that understand that I can mix hip hop into house, and vice versa. House is a great extension of disco, and hip hop owes a lot to disco too. If more people were educated in music, there wouldn't be so much ignorance when different types of music comes on.

Mark

I well remember the days (late 80s/ early 90s), when it was common practice for DJs to mix up the styles throughout a night. So you might have heard Steve Silk Hurley's 'Jack Your Body', followed by Public Enemy's 'Rebel Without A Pause', followed by Chaka Demus & Pliers 'Murder She Wrote' followed by Prince 'Kiss'—all from the same DJ!
Could we be seeing a gradual return to such open-mindedness? Or will the crowds continue to force pigeon-holing and categorisation on DJs?

Chippie,
(Croydon, England)

I think only a few years back R&B and hip hop music had a stigma attached to it, with regards to club owners associating it with large groups of black/ Asian boys kicking off when the music got a bit too 'heavy'. The thing is, this was usually the case! During this time the gulf got even bigger, and dance music would always be seen as the happy, chill-out vibe, which is good for the people making the money!

More recently, (within the last five years,) there has been the great 'urban' revival that has catapulted R&B and hip hop back into prime time club status. If it carries on the way it's going, we could be running side by side with the dance music DJs soon.

Belfast's Finest

I don't live in the mainland, (as the name would suggest), so I can't say anything about the trouble in urban nights as it's not a factor over here. However, I have a bit of an insight into the rest.

DJs'/ promoters' wages—simple. I worked for a dance music magazine/ events promotion company for a while. The reason these guys earn a fortune is because every single DJ had an agent. They were charging colossal money for pretty much fuck-all. As we know, it isn't a amazing skill being able to mix two records, (or three, or four,) for a length of time. An urban DJ can expect around £250 for a guest spot as there aren't many agents pushing us. Plus, if you're not from London—the perceived capital of urban—you've no mission.

Incidentally, have you ever tried to book an American artist for a PA? $6,000 plus plus rider, flights and hotels. The house scene got it right.

Exposure: In the urban scene, the press concentrates exclusively on the artists, and occasionally, the producer. Never the DJ's. In the house scene, the press concentrates on the DJs first, then the producers, and then the artists. As the majority of the DJs are also producers, it's self-serving. House music also has a majority bias towards electronic/ instrumental music, so this cuts out the need for artists.

Festivals: House festivals are based on the premise that the kids are going to be dancing for 12 hours to repetitive music. The drug of choice is ecstasy, which has the ability to turn normal punters into zombies; they will dance mindlessly in their own world causing no problems to others. The music is also geared towards gradual energy release, with warm-up sets ongoing throughout the earlier stages of the day, and then tougher sets at later stages. Electronic music festivals incorporate vastly different sounds also. Urban festivals are also based round the premise that the kids are going to be dancing for 12 hours, but a bit harder on coke and hash. Makes you a bit edgier, too. Plus, with egos at stake, every DJ tries to outdo the last, and ends up playing a similar set to the one before, who played a similar set to the one before, who played a simil...it goes on. There is no sense of 'warming up', so the euphoria is short-lived. There isn't a great deal of differentiation in urban music, it is vocal-based, (barring drum and bass, which isn't necessarily urban,) so hasn't room for expansion.

Branding: In the UK, our music is second fiddle, and non-London DJs mean fuck all, so how can a good club night get the exposure needed to develop successfully? I know there's some belters throughout the UK, but without radio or press exposure, (of which there is approximately zero), there's no chance.

Mark

Thanks for the insights. Some good points well made.

Regarding your opening comment about dance DJs charging so much because the agents are building in their own fees... the clubs always have the opportunity to refuse to pay such absurd sums. If all venues were to club together to demand this, the agents would be forced to drop their fees in order to achieve bookings for their acts.

You can be damn sure that promoters on the urban side would do this!

Belfast's Finest

I've had another thought about it, though. Dance DJs are booked on the basis that they have something different to offer; be it that they play a particular style of music, or they produce their own tracks and have had a hit, (underground or commercial).

What exactly do urban DJs offer at the minute? Turntablism, which is only appealing to a portion of the crowd, or crowd pleasing pop tracks.

Our music is the problem. Only a small portion of the crowd are into new and different music. The vast majority of R&B punters get their education from MTV. Dance punters are more discerning, it's sad to say.

Mark

There are a fair few R&B/ urban jocks that do make tunes, like their dance counterparts—but it rarely does them any good in increasing their profile at club level. Does anyone book Dodge because of his productions? Hell no—they book him 'cos he's done the MTV Licks and he's Trevor's mate!

**Bizzy,
(Bournemouth, England)**

Just read the opinions of Mark and Belfast's, and you both have solid points and have touched on the problems.

Dodge is one of the finest urban producers in this country. Just look at his resume—homeboy has remixed every interesting local and International urban act, and he doesn't get his props for that. If he was in the States, he'd be up there with the rest of them, but sadly he's not, so he has to keep playing in clubs and relying on MTV and being Trevor's mate to get his limited shine.

This links nicely with Belfast's opinion on the blatant and criminal way that MTV panders to commercial music, especially in the urban, (hate that word) area. This is my main beef with our music, the extent to which it's going mainstream nowadays.

I used to think that music stations existed to entertain and educate—entertain with good club songs, educate with new up and coming artists that might not blow up commercially, but still offer a good listen anyway. If you're unfortunate enough to watch MTV or any like-minded stations for a two-hour stretch, you'll see repeated plays for certain selected tracks time and time again.

Now, as a DJ, if you play a song in a club that's never been shown on these so-called 'urban' TV stations, you get a stuffy 18-21 year old girl or a chav male counterpart coming to tell you to change it and play Christina Aguilera's 'Dirrty' instead! (Incidentally, I remember a couple of years ago when the record label sent me 'Dirrty' three months before it got released and I played it in the club. I went on the mic and said to the crowd that they should trust me because this was going to be huge. Two minutes in, I got a tap on my shoulder by this girl telling me to change the music and play Nelly instead

'Dirrty' went to number one, of course, and I ended up getting requests every five minutes. This was exactly the same song I played prior to it charting, and nobody wanted to know. Suddenly it's on TV and it's cool? It bothers me a great deal.

Ever since BET Channel was stopped in '96 it has not been the same, in my opinion. Who remembers 'Rap City' and 'Good Vibrations' on that channel? it was a mix of mainstream and underground, and that's one of the things I still look forward to when I go to America.

Mark

This week, all the big movers and shakers of the dance music scene have been repping at the Winter Music 'Conference' in Miami, (though how many of them do you suppose actually attended any of the 'conferences? It's company expense accounts, penthouse suites and limos from the airport all the way.)

Can you imagine anything even coming close within the urban field, where all the big dogs of the UK R&B and hip hop scene assemble overseas for a week?

**DJ Hix,
Belfast, Northern Ireland**

Maybe this is off the topic a bit, but what in the hell is going on with Akon's new tune, 'Lonely'?

FEMALE DJS—WHAT DO WE THINK?

DJ D

Just interested to see what other people think about what it's like for female DJs working, or breaking into the R&B/ hip hop scene.

Talking about this, I've had mixed responses from people, some of them thinking that we've 'got it made', others understanding that our gender might actually work against us.

What do you think? What's it like in your area? Are there many/ any female DJs/ turntablists that you know of?

Lee Cocker
(Basildon, England)

Welcome to the forum! My opinion is that many female DJs are actually much better than the male ones, and that makes them feel threatened. It must be hard, because it has been a male-dominated arena for so long. But the female DJs that I have seen have blown the roof off the clubs that I have been to.

The best female hip hop/ R&B DJ I've seen is a girl called DJ Nicki, aka DJ Styles in Essex. She went on to form a group called Tommi, who had a track out a few months ago, but she kept up the DJing and was playing in London and on some radio stations. But I haven't heard much from her recently.

Mark

Sorry to say that I'm aware of at least half a dozen female DJs that are booked for their looks alone, and who have zero crowd-entertaining skills. Unfortunately, that's enough for a lot of sleazy club managers, who think it's good marketing to have a model-type behind the decks.

It means I have all the more respect for a female DJ who can truly cut it in what can be a fairly intimidating, male-dominated business. Hell, you get enough haters as a male. It must be even worse for a girl! So big respect to DJ D and all the other REAL female DJs putting it on out there. We need more of you!

DJ D

Great to read you responses guys. You've definitely hit a couple of the pressing issues, and much love for the support.

From my experience, especially starting when the scene was quite small, it ain't been easy. Lee, you're too right about the 'male-dominated' issue, and some fellas having trouble dealing with the possibility that a girl might give them a run for their money. Now that's not all the fellas, as some have shown great support. But still, I can't help but feel a little discriminated against sometimes.

And Mark, I agree 100 per cent about the skill factor. Although I played my first gig at the age of 11, I held off hitting the club scene for a few years after I was the legal age. I new that some promoters would use the female factor as a marketing tool, and didn't want to become the 'flavour of the month'.

Turning down an offer for one of the best residencies in Sydney, I locked myself in my studio and practiced every opportunity available. I'm so glad that I did, because every time something could potentially go wrong, my skills have helped me hold it down. It's forced a few fellas to lift their game, and funnily enough, a few of them have come back to me and asked for lessons.

DJ Geespot

Good topic, D, and I'll have to agree with MD when he says some of the female DJs are just a marketing/ hype tool, rather than real entertainers.

However, I have seen some women DJs who are really good when it comes to spinning. The problem is they always get playa-hated by male DJs. I remember a gig in Durban where a male DJ broke the female DJ's needle because he saw that the crowd was responding more to her mixes than his own. when the male was mixing. Some guys just can't take a bit of competition, in which case, why are you in the business?!

Tony T, aka 'Embassy'
(London, England)

Well I take the point that a lot of these female DJ's are just eye candy, one I actually know a few that can DJ just as good or better than most DJ's. Notably DJ Noora, DJ Rapture and DJ Babyblu.

Without seeing these people play you will think they are good. Babyblu has some amazing mixes, she flew out to Athens and ripped it with the Hiphop,RnB and Ragga. She has DJ'd for a host of people US and Uk notably Klashnekoff in the UK. If you watched the MOBO's she DJ'd for Mos Def when he did his track 'Sex Love and Money'. She has cut for GZA and Ghostface and the listening party for Nas' album (Hot album!!)

In the end of the day she wipes the floor with all the 'eye-candy' DJ's she don't dress to impress she just goes down to do her work and she is good at her profession.

If you don't know about her, you should go down to Deal Real, Carnaby street London(nearest Tube, Oxford Circus) where you will see her playing for most of the notable acts who come to the Uk and from the UK.

Don't judge a DJ by how thy look but by how they play.

Unfortunately this industry is fucked, we are living in the MTV generation, people no longer listen to quality music they are influenced by the video hence the reason Jill Scott, Angie Stone are not as big as Ashanti.

What I like right now is the fact Mos Def's album is number 4 in the US Billboards with no advertisement and video as of yet, just by the music. I am sure his acting may have played a part but that is damn big without the music marketing.

One

Tony

Mark

A DJ should only ever be judged on how they perform, rather than how they look. Same thing for artists. Unfortunately, in a world indoctrinated and obsessed by marketable images, it's rarely the case!

Belfast's Finest

Let's be honest here, there are that few female DJ's in the scene that any girl with a record collection and a nice smile could get club gigs... it's all about marketing, isn't it?? I'm not going to name names but the few female DJ's i've heard have been at best mediocre.

Sad but true

Molf
(Gaborone, Botswana)

Let the female dJ's enter the scene guyz,its long time since the scene has been dominated by guys,and its good to have new female dJ's coming up,and bringing some changes to the game,and i also believe that we should not judge them by their looks,but by their performance.

Lee Drummond

Sounds to me like there are a lot of guys out there that cannot hack it when it comes to competition from the opposite sex...WELCOME ALL DJs...regardless of creed, colour and of course SEX. If you can play it, mix it and perform for the crowd, the bring it on. I want to see more female DJs as well as hear them...its all good playing the tracks that make the crowd go crazy...but I still prefer the DJ that talks to the crowd.. a silent DJ is an anonymous one...if you are trapped in the DJ booth that is hidden away then the punter can't get to know you and feel that vibe that can only be created when you speak to us...if the voice on the mike is a powerful FEMALE...now that is a DJ with a difference and the rest of the ladies in the club will feel a bigger part of the world that has been male dominated for too long.

This is not a profession that ONLY MALES CAN DO!!! The women are the biggest requesters of tracks in a club, so we know they know their music...so if they know what they want to hear I am sure they know how to play it to get the crowds going. If you are a good MALE Dj then why should you be SCARED of a FEMALE DJ??? Show them your stuff and they will show you their own.. and maybe you might just learn something new...I welcome them to centre stage...but I wanna hear you not just see you. OK...If you look sexy...then there will always be an element of exploitation...but so what...we all do it..male and female alike...if a guy looks good..as a DJ..the ladies love hime..so ladies..use what you got!!!

Its not sexist...its your right as a human...in the clubs and on the radio...lets get more women..sorry...ladies out there on the DJ scene...

Mark

Show them your stuff and they'll show you theirs? Sounds good!

Sorry—forgive the Benny Hill moment there. Good point about DJs chatting on the mic. Maybe that's a discussion topic in itself? As Mighty MP points out, many otherwise competent DJs are too afraid to talk to their crowd, whereas I've always considered it to be an essential [artr of being an all-round skilled DJ.

DJ DAs Mighty MP points out, many otherwise competent DJs are too afraid to talk to their crowd, whereas I've always considered it to be an essential part of being an all-round skilled DJ.

Just a quick one to express my appreciation of Lee's attitude in his post earlier on. I agree with pretty much all of what you've said, and am grateful for you taking the time to say it!

Happy 2 say that the scene is changing here in Sydney & that I have been teaching guys how to spin for the last couple yrs. I still get treated differently in a lot of situations to the fellas, however it is all part of the job, and you learn to deal with it in one way or another.

I have also been known 2 pick up the mic at my gigs, although I haven't done that 4 a bit.. Regardless, I speak to the crowd with my gestures, hand movements etc..

+ even jump in there with them for a boogie.. as well as dancing on the tables while spinning, shaking their hands, giving them T-shirts/ caps/ CDs/etc, and chatting with them. It's more than just playing, it's about stage presence & performing for the crowd, & at the same time being yourself & giving them what they want. I'll do whatever I can 2 get them hyped.

so much for a 'quick one'

Mark

Just interested to know, D, in your DJ escapades, do you get much bitchiness from girl punters? Or do they tend not to bother you at all, and all the grief comes from the guys?

**DJ Queen T
(London, England)**

Interesting hearing your views/comments! I'm one half of the Mixtresses (female DJ duo) and we're fairly new to the UK scene, only been DJ-ing about 2 yrs now, and work full time jobs as well—so in all honesty we don't spend as much time as we'd like perfecting our skills!!

But I think the reason we get booked and re-booked by promoters is firstly our tune selection, which we make a big effort to tailor to the crowd, high energy and interaction/fun with the crowd that we bring to a gig (well we hope so anyway...!)

I think marketing is increasingly important in this competitive industry and we've worked hard in branding the Mixtresses name/image (check our site www.mixtresses.co.uk) and promoters have to look for something different to make their nights stand out from others and in some cases a female DJ can add this to their event...

We don't compare ourselves to other female DJ's who are HOT skills-wise on the decks (sounds like you're one of them DJ D!) but we know we can keep even the most difficult crowds moving and we have a great time with the other DJ's/ppl we meet along the way...Mark you know what we're talking about!

Being female has made it both harder and easier for us to break in to the industry—you have to prove yourself a lot more (especially to other male DJ's) and also deal with the 'haters' who think you're only booked for your breasts and booty (ahem!)

I think there's enough room for everyone, our feeling is that it's important to have fun with it and support each other—we've all heard some rubbish male and female DJ's play so it's great if we can give everyone a chance and not judge anyone based on their gender, but what they bring into the mix...!

xx

Mark

Thanks for the comments, T. I was hoping we could get word from The Mixtresses on this! For anyone who don't now, these girls are definitely putting it on on the London party scene, playing just about every spot in town on the regular.

As T says, it's the DJs that put the effort into marketing themselves that stand to gain the most profile as a result. It's about so much more than just being hot on the decks. If nobody gets to hear about what you're doing, you're nowhere! On this note, be sure to check the Mixtresses' website. There are so many DJs out there who still don't have one!

Random

Right I am not a DJ, rapper, or anything to do with the industry!

Im a guy inda streetz! So hopefully my opinion is helpful and wanted???????

Ever since my youth I have been heavily into the HipHop/Rap and RnB scenes, music, clothing, lifestyle...u name it I did it. (yes EVERYTHING)

I am very selective about what I consider a club banger! Regardless of the commercialness of a particular track. DJ's Male/Female now seem to be just interested in whats the Top Ten Chart...and they think that playing these tracks will please the crowd...Not exactly. Sure its great to hear track that are given great amounts of Radio Play today, however its the Golden Oldies/Blasts from the Pasts/ Emotional Tracks that get the soul shakin' on the dance floor in my opinion. If I had a choice to go to a night out in a New RnB gig or Old Skool gig, the latter would win hands down...but hey that's just my opinion.

Now I have had the pleasure of following one of London's Female DJ Duo, by the name of The Mixtresses (Damn Hotties I tell ya), they're into R&B/ Rare Grooves/ Mild Hip Hop and it is due to their extensive(all most exhaustive) knowledge of tunes dating back to early 90's that make them a winner in my books.

Over two years I have covered their tracks from starting up to residencies they now have...and I must agree with DJ D and Mark --> First impressions are that they are doing what they are doing simply cos they got the looks. Yeah true they are fine lasses...however my argument is as follows;

1) How come every time these girls end up starting a set at their residency's, the crowd cheers (no joke)...it

can't be cos they are familiar with the DJs (not everyone in the club...could it be . This behaviour really does set the atmosphere to BUZZIN inside a club. I reckon its cos of their Unique Mixtresses Dub! Nice familiar Justin Timberlake tune, with a twist of ragga...ingenious!

2) The sets they are playing are so-so-so bespoke its unbelievable. Where else can you hear a set you heavy + varied with tracks such as Juicy-Biggie to Love that Your Givin—Gwen McGrey to Jodeci—Cry For you? I have yet to find any DJ (Male/Female) that varies their track selection as much as these girls do. Now I think this is what sets these girls apart from the rest of the Female DJ crowd in London. Most of the competition have the looks granted, some are even more highly skilled, but from a punter's point of view...its all about the MUSIC <-- 'na what am sayin? Ladies have more of aptitude to please ALL, rather than a specific set of individuals. My point is I think Male DJs still have nothing to worry about, but with REAL talent from Female DJ's such as The Mixtresses, you can no longer say that its all a hype being a Female DJ. Still think I'm wrong, book ur next gig to be that where the Mixtresses will be playing and find out for yourself.

Laterz Amigos!

*

BOUNCERS. WHY?

Mark

The best way to set the scene for this one is the following extract from my website Diary, concerning an encounter with bouncers at a recent gig in Scotland.

'The club's door staff could be described as many things. Let's be diplomatic and stick to 'over-zealous'. Having located the place, I proceeded to take a quick picture of the exterior for this site. Immediately, one of the bouncers rushed across the road and asked what I was doing. It was tempting, but I stuck to a sensible answer, explaining who I was... but what did the guy think he was going to do? It's a nightclub, not a military installation. What authority does he have to stop me? When I stepped up to the front door to await the promoter, another 'security operative' then told me I couldn't leave my record case where I'd put it as it was 'obstructing a public thoroughfare'. I suggested he show me where he'd prefer me to put it, and he moved it about a foot to the left. Ah, door staff. Aren't they priceless?!

This is only one of countless stories I could relate regarding bouncers and the incredible power trips they embark on... and I know every DJ and punter out there must have a thousand more '

DJ Geespot

I think the problem with most of the bouncers that I've come across is that they think people don't respect their job, and thus they should instil law and order every time, even when it's unnecessary. I once went to play in a place outside PE, and I got there early so I could check with the promoter what time I'd be playing. I told the bouncers who I was, but they said I'd have to wait in line just like everyone else. The fact that I'd told them I was there to work as a DJ didn't mean sh*t to them. I had to call the promoter to get him out of the venue, and while I was waiting, the bouncers kept insinuating that I shouldn't be standing next to the door. The problem with them is that they never care to find out anything about who might be playing that night. All they want is people to listen to them, and they're more than happy to resort to physical force if you don't.

Mark

Are people just trying to be politically correct here and keep their jobs?! C'mon, man. Everyone's got a bouncer story, right?!

DJ D

Yup, everyone has a story. Fortunately, as of late, mine have been good! (Is it a female thing?) I've been lucky enough to even get the odd few bouncers offering to carry my crates without even asking them.

I find here in Aus, if you've got a record crate with you, there are no probs. Without one, though, you're forced to line up just like anyone else.

Here's a good one for you, though. I was the support at the KCI & Jojo concert, and when attempting to go to the after-party on the second night was refused entry, even though I had a performer's pass. Now, that was whack, and a prime example of where bouncers' 'egos' or power trips can get in the way.

Another interesting fact. In the Middle East a fella can't walk into a club without a female. A hard one, considering a good number of the females don't go out. (Maybe this is why there are only two clubs in the whole Sultanate of Oman??)

Mark

Yeah, here in the UK, a lot of clubs don't let more than two males in at a time unless they've got two or more females with them. Stops the place becoming too 'manned up' and 'thugged out' in their eyes.

On the subject of walking past bouncers with a record case, that's always struck me as a brilliant blag to get into a club where you're not actually playing. Just waltz up with a record bag over your shoulder, say 'alright mate' to the bouncers as you stroll confidently past... then check your bag in at the cloakroom and enjoy a free night's clubbing! Never tried it myself, but I know people who have!

Geespot

Yeah, I've done the crate thing, man. Playing in one club, and after I finish, I just go to the next club and tell them I've been booked to play there too. Like I said, bouncers never care to ask or know a bit about the DJ who'll be coming to play, so I use it to my advantage!

Molf

These guys are always rude to everyone. They're like someone who gatecrashes a party and then takes control of everything without knowing or even caring whose party it was in the first place!

I mean, I blame the promoters/ clubs. Why can't they make these guys aware of who'll be performing? A photograph might help. It sucks when you get harassed by a bouncer and you've got just as much right to be there as them!

Mark

Hmmmm. Not many people willing to lay into bouncers here. Is it because they're generally a decent bunch who don't deserve the grief?

Doorbitch
(North East England)

I am a female bouncer based in the North East of England, and just want to give you some info.

Most door staff are okay, and as long as you explain to them why you are there and what you are doing, they will let you in the venue without having to stand in line. Be aware, though, that the door staff are hardly ever notified by management who is playing, and when we get to work, there are normally no management or staff around who know what day it is, let alone what's happening that night at the venue.

Even if we are told, on most occasions, there are a number of people playing at the venue on the same night, and remembering names that we have never heard of is difficult.

Also, we get a lot of people coming up to us saying 'I'm with the DJ', or claiming to be the DJ when they actually aren't.

Remember, our job is pretty tough, and I don't reckon many of you would lay in to us face-to-face! I'm not being arsey, but you try doing our job!

Mark

Fair enough. Thanks for the input!

UK VIP Pimp
(Midlands, England)

Fair enough??!

I think you will find that anyone walking through the door of the club would constitute part of the doorperson's job.

Any door person should make every effort to find out who is performing at your venue. If you don't, you're quite simply failing to do your job properly. Period!

Roffie
(Leamington Spa, England)

I quit a residency at a venue due to one of the door staff. He used to harass my girlfriend every time she came over to watch me play. When she brought it to my attention, I confronted him about it. He decided to turn nasty on me because he couldn't have her. The last straw came when he saw me with my girlfriend in the club and knocked our drinks over. Obviously, physically challenging this meathead was a non-starter. The management denied his actions, so I quit.

Mark

Anyone remember a classic UK rave record from about 1992 by Kicks Like A Mule called 'The Bouncer'? The central hook features a rough-sounding doorman saying, 'your name's not down, you're not coming in.'

It was as relevant then as it is today!

Karl Cross,

Two words for the UK readers ... Fran Cosgrave!

If you're not familiar, he was a bouncer for a pop band, and he recently won a 'reality' TV show called 'Celebrity Love Island'! He worked in club near me recently as a 'DJ'. He was paid £4,000 for a set and can be quoted for saying "I'm making money now while I can, I'll be nobody in a few months." Or words to that effect!

Says it all. Bouncers aren't celebrities!

THE R&B CLUB SCENE: GOING DOWN THE TUBE?!

Mark

This one comes from Wayne McDonald, one of the North East's most prolific DJs/ producers, as part of his latest report for Blues & Soul mag's Clubhoppin'. It speaks for itself, and it's certainly food for thought. What do we all think?

*

And finally—my main point. Or 'The Sermon According To Wayne': The recent mixed fortunes of the once extremely popular Thursday nights at LoveDough (Ikon, Newcastle) are raising many an eyebrow, amid speculation that the R&B bubble is finally starting to burst and return to a level of normality once again, after the entire UK witnessed a rather hasty transformation of many socialite types to the bling bling world of ghetto gangsterizm, making nites like 'LoveDough' across the country so accessible and fashionable.

I'm not intending to have a go at the LoveDough team here, because against the odds they went on to build up one of the biggest R&B nights in the North East region; I'm merely using their nite to illustrate my point.

Across the country, we are starting to experience another transition—an audience shrinkage—because the urban music scene reached almost saturation point with 'street music' supposedly readily available almost everywhere—albeit in its most diluted, commercial forms. Thus, the cultural chameleons at many of these styled events are now heading away from the R&B scene to adapt themselves into whatever 'the next big thing' may be. Its gonna be up to us—the regions tastemakers who helped build up our regional 'scenes' in the first place—to revamp ourselves and the music we play.

Lets not become complacent, and play all the hits that can be found on compilation albums or heard on daytime radio day in, day out. But lets get back to work and continue to break in the new music, which will help maintain that level of interest that we have all worked so hard to create. If we don't act now, be warned: across the country, we'll soon be seeing loads more R&B casualties—of this I am sure.

Belfast's Finest

I can honestly say I've never been more unhappy DJing as I have this last year. I've had to play music I vowed I would never play to keep people dancing, and the crowds go to new lows when it comes to requests. The scene is stagnant, and the music coming out of America does little to alleviate the situation—the vast majority of 'bling' hip-hop being trite with no value in it's content (I'm fed up of hearing about each new rapper talking about new products or their fake gangster lives, or shit pop acts 'ooh'ing & 'aah'ing with no real feeling) , and real music continues to remain ignored.

I've been faced with 3 choices:
  - take the money (which I've had to do—pays the bills)
  - look elsewhere for musical satisfaction (joined a soul collective, at least once a month I can play different music with feeling)
  - give it all up (which I'm considering)

Mark

Well, number three's an option. But somehow I don't think you'll do it. As DJs, the music, and the culture that goes with it is in our blood. Is there anything else you could do where you'd truly be happy?

Number one is something I'm sure every DJ in the land an relate to! It's this thought that keeps me going through some of my less desirable DJ sets. (No names mentioned!)

David Craig
(Dubai, UAE)

Great point made by Wayne also feeling Belfast's grumble. But in all honesty most of us have never been so busy or so well paid , granted for sometimes having to play more commercial stuff. Surely there's always the option to mix it up with more upfront tracks or old skool anthems. It's to easy to blame the crowd for your own complacency. Okay it's a pain having teenage girls asking for dirty and you can do it but c'mon you are getting paid to play music it could be allot worse.

Sometimes I think the DJs could be a bit more adventurous and stop relying on the same old tried and tested set. Yeah the scene has been over exposed and saturated and like Wayne said it will probably to some extent revert back to how it used to be. But I don't think that's necessarily a bad thing. Those part time house and pop DJs can go back to where they came from and leave the real heads to do their thing. albeit on a slightly smaller scale than before.

Mark

It's true that back in the day, the most that we urban jocks could expect from a club was a back room session in the mid-week. At least now there are opportunities to play main room sets every weekend. The price to pay is having to water down the music—but there's a price to pay for most things in life!

So if, as Wayne suggests, our scene gets driven back to becoming a more specialist thing, we have to balance the artistic satisfaction of being able to play more meaningful music, with the limited financial prospects it would bring.

Tough one...

Belfast's Finest

David, I'm not complacent—I've always tried to break new & different music; I'm a music fan, that's why I got into this in the first place. I've always tried hard to slip new music into the mix—it's just the ratio's have been increasing; 5 years ago you could play 1 new to 1 well-known track, now you'd be lucky to slip a new track in amongst 10 'pop' tracks.

Also, the average punter gets their music knowledge from MTV, and is likely to be under 20, so I find it extremely hard to play anything over 3 years old without fear of thinning out the dancefloor. Something like Tweet 'Boogie 2nite' would be considered old-school; a frightening prospect.

If you're lucky enough to play to more open-minded crowds, fair play to you, mate

Mark

True dat. I played Biggie 'One More Chance' in a student jam recently. Some girls came up and asked me to stop playing 'this old crap', and play 'some R&B instead.'

What can you say?

Guest

I agree with Wayne, we do have to take more risks and break more music... problem is that in the current climate if we do, we will all lose our jobs to joey bedroom urban jock who will play the hits for £50. fact.

to Belfast's finest. i hear you. i have never been so bored with the urban scene. so much so that i have started doing nu jazz/ jazz/broken beats nights which are now my favourite nights and i am getting that good feeling when choosing my tunes again. i hate to say it but on some urban nights i actually think to myself "which tunes do i hate the most" cos those are the ones that the public love.

it's a difficult problem cos i am being paid to entertain and i kinda feel bad moaning about it cos i earn good money and i am playing loads of nights and it certainly beats working 9 to 5 in a job i hate but, come on, playing Beyoncé, Destiny's Child, Usher and 50 Cent every night is pretty boring. some nights i could play last weeks cd and they would love it!!!

wouldn't it be great if we could be more adventurous. to David, i want to come and play where you are cos adventurous in Bristol means heading for the door with your bags packed. for every adventurous tune i play i get 20 rude obnoxious annoying women [oh yeah its you women out there who bitch moan and complain the most] telling me to play...wait for it...i know you've heard it too...something more [god i hate this word] UPTEMPO...there, i've said it. do people in the UK actually know what UPTEMPO means?

i like to do a little test on these women. when i get pressure to play something more uptempo i will deliberately play slower tracks but the slower i get the more well known the song is. this always works as you then see these annoying women shaking their thing on the floor. for god sake, ask for what you really want. just come up to me and say BRAD CAN YOU PLAY THE SAME OLD BORING CRAP THAT EVERYONE ELSE PLAYS, YOU KNOW THE SHIT I HEAR ON THE RADIO AND SEE ON MTV, YOU KNOW THE SONGS THAT ME AND MY GIRLFRIENDS CAN SING ALONG TO ON THE DANCEFLOOR.

R&B isn't dying. its been dead a long time...

**Bobby Speed
(Bristol, England)**

Mark—that last rant was from me by the way and what the hell am i doing up at 8.30 !!!!

Mark

Just what I was wondering...

Karl Cross

Hi Guys,

A lot a valuable points in all your posts, I agree with Belfasts 1 in 10 new tunes. These days I'm getting such a mixed crowd too, It's different from one week to the next. I know a DJ's job is to educate in a lot of cases, but you cant if the pupils don't want to learn.

Girlies always come and ask for "you can do it", "crazy in love" and god help us "Justin". Now I know that if I play these, my harder fans will leave the floor. If I play newer stuff "50's Candy Shop (not too heavy!)" etc, the girls leave and I end with a floor full of Hip Hop Hedz, which I like (but the management don't!). Then theres the final mob, who like "Next's Wifey, Jaheim, Peaches & Cream" that scares off the others cos "its too old" or "not hard enough"

It seems from what I've witnessed lately around this region, people like what they like and its hard to teach them different. And with local radio stations (none specified) playing their so called "Urban Chart" which is just full of rubbish, (cos they got an interview) and presented by someone looking like a McFly reject who cant mix Flour & Water, what chance do the real DJ's get?

But what can you do, It pays my bills too!

KC

Mark

And the worrying thing is, this seems to be a trend throughout the UK. It's the same story whatever region you look at.

Guest

Bobby Speed—I'm doing exactly the same thing; I play a night once a month dropping broken beat, nu-jazz, nu-soul & deep house!! Mad how you have to move away from the music you were brought up with because of commercialism; sucks balls.

I was DJing with a pop star last night (booked for a DJ set to pick up crowds which had been dropping). He was pretty crap, but the teenage girls were going mad because of who he is—I came on after he'd finished, and half the crowd disappeared to follow him, get autographs etc. If this is indicative of what is happening to our scene, well fuck it, I don't want to be a part of it anymore.

Bizzy
Guest

I have read all yr posts and cant stop laughing because all what y'all said is true, if you guys that play out think deeply, you will notice that you are now playing at home more that you normally use to, i have now noticed that every time i get back from a gig, hit home and get to bed, i cant wait to get up the next day to hit my decks at home, its like i am exorcising the demons from the night before as most of the records i play at clubs, dont go anywhere near my decks at home, why cant everybody just be like me and listen to GOOD MUSIC, do most people know that the most criminally slept on album(rock, heavy metal, trance, hip hop, r&b, bashment whatever) last year was Pete Rock's SOUL SURVIVOR 2. i am seriously considering having a party at mine every weekend and only true heads show up.

Sam Young

I agree with what a lot of you are saying, punters in the clubs get most of their knowledge from commercial radio and MTV. Last night I was DJing and I was playing 'regulate' by warren g and some guy asked me to play some r+b and hiphop ?????

thats not the 1st time either, but hey I dont expect everyone to be a anorak in music like most DJs.

the best way I find breaking new records is to squeeze them between well known joints and try and do it as much as possible.

but at the end of the day were getting paid to play music and give people a good time, life could be much harder !

Mark

Is it just me, or do situations like that 'Regulate' scenario bring about an uncharacteristic violent streak and make you want to bottle the person concerned?

Ah , just me then ... Hmmm.

Belfast's Finest

'Regulate' is hardly an anorack's choice; up until about 2 years ago you could play that anywhere and heads would bob knowingly; now the teenyboppers (the 17 to 19 year olds who make up 90% of the club crowd) who have hijacked the scene have ruined it, you can't play any classics for fear of clearing the floor.

Mind you, that's not an issue for me; I've just lost my last regular R'n'B gig due to good old club politics; and to be perfectly honest, I'm not upset about it. My day job covers the bills, and the infrequent gigs I get playing nu-soul & broken beats gives me pocket money ... suits me fine; I get to play music I ACTUALLY LIKE to punters who ACTUALLY LIKE IT!!!!!!!!!

Mark

Your position will actually be viewed as quite an enviable one by DJs who rely on spinning for their full-time income!

There seems to be a general trend emerging throughout the UK towards venues starting to drop R&B/ urban nights like they're hot again. I'm not entirely sure what's driving this, but I've had a number of DJ friends moaning to me in recent weeks that they're finding it harder and harder to get work. In my own experience, a lot of venues and promoters are trying to get me to cut down on my money—not that I'm anywhere near as expensive as some I could mention! Maybe it's just a financial issue, or maybe it's deeper rooted?

Anyone else finding this?

Belfast's Finest

It's r'n'b that's killed it for the DJ—it's pop music; which club worth it's salt wants to put on pop nights?? Also, r'n'b isn't what the kids want anymore; rock is the big sound—I played a party on Friday night and was tortured to play rock music; R'n'B was ok for some of the girls, but the vast majority wanted Franz Ferdinand, the Killers, Oasis etc...

I wasn't rubbing it in either about me having a full-time job; I've only just got permanent work after years of trying to pay the bills with DJ work & part-time jobs; any time I relied on the DJing solely it seemed my work offers would dry up. I'm just in a happier position now were I don't have to rely on DJing to pay bills, so can concentrate on playing music I like.

Mark

That's all good, man. You do what you gotta do, and different options work for different people. If you've found a situation that's good for you, then more power to you!

Interesting comment about the rock music...an unsettling thought!

Belfast's Finest

Yeah, it disturbed me too, I'm not exactly a fan. It wasn't half obvious tho, rock hasn't been as big with kids since the early 90's. It's also more accessible; when tossers like 50 are yapping on about whatever new product they want to endorse, rock music is more in tune with kids feelings.

This could be a good thing tho—there'll be split in the scene between 'real' soul and the pop shit scene.

Mark

Last night, I dropped Amerie's 'One Thing', in my opinion, the funkiest, most soulful tune to have appeared in the past year, an absolute belter, and a surefire hit as soon as it gathers enough momentum. A few people stood bemused and motionless on the dancefloor before walking off.

I then played Kelis 'Milkshake'—probably for the 250th time in my life. Floor packs out.

A small incident, but it says so much...

*

R&B CLUBS—CRISIS POINT AGAIN?

Mark

Anyone who's been in the game for a few years will know that the R&B/ urban club scene goes around in cycles. It passes through good phases and not-so-good phases all the time.

However, there does appear to be something going on that's affecting clubs throughout the land right now, and it does seem to give cause for concern.

As has been discussed at length in other sections of this forum, the lines between R&B and pop music have become so blurred, that they're now virtually the same thing. Although this has had its benefits for R&B DJs so far, in creating many work opportunities for those prepared to water down their sets, it now seems to be the case that venue managers are dropping R&B/ urban events like they're hot. The logic is that the average commercial/ chart/ cheese set in any High Street venue now contains such a high quota of 'R&B', that clubs no longer need to be marketing specific nights.

As a result, real R&B DJs are now finding resistance from clubs when it comes to trying to do something meaningful with the music. I've been getting reports of this from Scotland, Northern Ireland, the Midlands, the North East and the South East...so it appears to be a widespread trend.

Nothing is easy in our game. Here's another hurdle for us well-meaning but hard-pressed DJs to overcome!

Guest

R&B nights throughout the country are struggling in general, especially the Friday night ones...just look at how many Ministry get in nowadays compared to 3 years ago...in the past 2 years since I've been going we started off at 800 through the door with residents, and now struggle to get 400 apart from the monthly slot where we have a guest which attracts up to 1000 plus guests...its not that we are doing anything wrong music wise, in fact i think rnb and hiphop is particularly strong about now with loads of big tunes out...its just that people are just not raving like they used too...everyone thinks it will come back around but as far as i can see that will not be for some time...if ever.

 the following are to blame...
 playstations and home entertainment
 rising house prices

drink price wars amoungst rival bars
  too many licences being granted for new bars

**Tony Amore
(London, England)**

I think coming from an MC or clubbers point of view this situation can be used as a benefit. Now real R&B nights can be organised because all fans of the music know that these stardard nights always have the same overplayed tunes without a chance to play quality R&B you wont here from a pop DJ dabbling with the genre. This means though, the real DJ's need to be on point and can't be lazy and play the tunes we hear every week in the pub. We need more nights to be a blend of forgotten classics and quality modern gems.

If promoters do their homework and offer a different night for club owners to get into then I believe they'll go for it and real DJ's will be like gold dust. I reckon all club owners want is a chance to have a rammed club with a whole range of different punters paying admission fees, buying drinks that you couldn't achieve with just a copy of the lasted R&B compilation cd on repeat.

Mark

I hope you're right, man. I would love that sort of scenario to come around. Sounds a little too close to Utopia right now, though!

Mark

This is in the latest Blues & Soul mag report from Wayne C McDonald in the North East. I think it neatly encapsulates everything:

...and finally, a quick word if i may. Without wishing to patronise anybody or nothing, but its happening as i said, isn't it? The scene is getting more difficult with more R&B club nite casualties by the day. Look how many times our friends have looked us in the eye and said "There's nowhere left to go out," even though there's R&B music being blasted from just about every single nook and cranny. "The music ain't what it used to be." Is this down to the DJs, the music or are punters taste's just changing, as forecasted. I personally think its a mix of all three elements. When are jocks gonna realise that people can only respond to what they hear?

Too many DJs are getting lazy and only playing the tracks they see on the likes of MTV Base and Channel U, whilst sitting on a whole host of quality tracks that have yet to have televised exposure. Thinking back to when the scene was smaller, we could play what we wanted how we wanted to our relative crowds, because they were thirsty and hungry for the soul food. Today, as we reach R&B saturation point, there's only so much of the commercial crop of music that people want to hear before boredom comes into play. And once people get bored, they leave without wishing to return in a hurry. So what can we do?

The only thing left to help us is ourselves. A larger selection of our punters than we realise want to listen to new material to ensure they get a different sonic experience whenever they visit our club nites, instead of the regular No Diggedy, Fatman Scoop and Ice Cube soundtrack that the £30 a nite bandwagon jocks are still spinning. In all honesty, I ain't expecting no overnight miracles. But, with a softly softly approach, we can ALL become players again. All it takes is just being that little more braver to throw in a brand new track here and there that YOU actually like, in the hope of spreading some of your feelgood factor music.

So what if you lose a few from the dance floor? You'll soon be able to drag them back by dropping some current biggie. The more newies we can get away with, whilst also playing a few others that your crowd may have forgotten about from back in the day, will soon have your punters in soul heaven. This fresh approach will help to keep the fires burning and begin to fan the flames of R&B passion once again!

And you can trust me on that...

Guest

Mark you have a point there. I'm an RnB/DJ promoter in the Midlands & I have had more knock backs from clubs nowadays about running RnB nights. In my hometown the council has passed an order to the clubs NOT to have dedicated RnB nights or their licences are at risk. Since that order was passed, the clubbing numbers have dropped to less than half the capacity on a Friday. The Pop DJs are also not doing the genre any favours as the belt out the same over played RnB tunes & never progress their sets. It is a sad state of affairs. Its now getting harder to give proper feedback my mailing lists as most of the tracks Im sent dont get reactions until they are being played on radio or MTV Base.

Freeview music channels I feel are partially to blame in not educating the public about what RnB really is & where it came from. e.g. their definition of ultimate RnB tunes are things like Gwen Stefani , come on!!!

Mark

I'm so tired of hearing about councils and local authorities banning R&B or urban nights on the basis that they lead to trouble. Let's have some consistency then. I want to see house, techno and drum 'n' bass nights being shut down too, in that case, on the basis that all the punters are doing mind-altering substances that make them moody and prone to fight.

But of course that never happens.

Belfast's Finest

But the drugs will melt their minds, therefore making them more compliant with Uncle Tony's restrictive legislation he plans to bring through...Anyway, have you been at a techno night; it's worse than line-dancing—all those funboys...

Never mind banning urban nights; they should ban stupid birds going to urban nights; they should be forced to name their 3 favourite songs of all time, and anyone mentioning Britney or Christina should be turned away...

Mark

Anyone naming Christina's 'Dirty' should be given a lethal injection on the spot.

Belfast's Finest

Any girl asking for 'Dirrty' is usually looking for an injection, whether it's lethal or not depends on her attitude toward protection

UK VIP Pimp

this situation AGAIN....i remember doing a night with MD @ THE PLACE (when it existed) last time the pop/r&b thing was going on. the only thing the REAL DJs can do is play through it! the night i did with MD attracted only the REAL urban crowd due to its reputation. these people only came out to hear the latest or greatest beats, it made our jobs real enjoyable, you would walk out of a rave with a stupid smile on your face, knowing you just blitzed the masses and you knew they would all be back when YOU returned to play! this still happens in places, you just have to look... HARD!!!

we all know that it will clean up again one day. but as already mentioned, we just gotta keep educating, they will eventually realise that the DJ they are hearing is not only a DJ... he's a teacher!

so...

Mark

Yeah, man, it's just a case of riding through the rocky patches and coming out the other side. It's happened many times before. It's sure to happen again.

**Lil Kriss P
(Essex, England)**

Too true. its harder now than it ever has been cos we are now past the crest of a wave. I remember speaking to Mark about it at Tiger Tiger up here in Newcastle, and i speak to Wayne on the regular and everyone is in agreement than what we as DJs need to do, is a) break new music (first and foremost!) and b) on a more personal level, try to cultivate a British scene that can compete with the US juggernaut. better go, out DJing at 8. peace up, N-toon doon. LKP

Mark

Don't you just love August? It's the time of year when that ever-popular phrase, 'we'll leave it til October when the students come back' can be heard from every promoter's/venue manager's mouth!

*

SMOKING IN CLUBLAND

Mark

Following the lead of California, New York and Ireland, it's becoming increasingly likely that the UK government will eventually impose a ban on smoking in all workplaces—which of course includes restaurants, bars and nightclubs.

While this can be applauded on health grounds, how worried should DJs, promoters and venue owners be about the likely effect this will have on numbers? In a country where punters certainly love their fags, will this cause people to stay away in their droves?

Or will clubs lay on special outdoor spaces where smokers can step out to get their fix? What do you think?

DJ Geespot

Well in South Africa buildings are supposed to provide smoking areas..So if the UK authority can do the same thing and give the smokers a chance I have no beef.I mean there is no point in totally banning smoking,coz right now the big sponsors for different sports codes,like F1 for eg are cigarette companies..I know smoking is bad and it can affect passive smokers but its not right to imprison smokers..

The DJs and promoters should not be that worried,but for smoking djs I dont know…I think there will put into consideration the good side of smoking first..

Mark

I hadn't even thought about DJs who like a smoke/ toke while they're spinning. Guess they'll either have to draw for the Nicotine patches, or find another job!

DJ Geespot

Or just stop smoking Nicotine patches wont work all the time.Addiction or rather craving is a state of mind, and people can get through it...

Mark

I've just got back from Dublin, where the smoking ban has now been in place for several months. Clubbers there have totally adapted to the situation, and it doesn't seem to have been bad for business at all. The Vaults, where I play, allows smokers to step outside to a designated area to get their fix on, then come straight back in with a hand stamp. As long as all venues in the UK were to adopt a similar approach should the ban happen there, all should be cool.

It makes a real difference leaving at the end of the night and not smelling like an old ashtray!

Molf

smoking in da club sucks guyz, i really like the idea coz,u know if u are a non smoker the guyz wanna blow tha shit on ya! and u get outta the club like u been doin that yourself,so it will actually help us smell better coz i hate the smell of a cigarette myself and when someone does it next to me my breath chokes.

Mark

Point taken!
 I think it's an inevitable thing in the UK, in the name of political correctness!

Molf

The law is above us guys,so there is nothing we can do,lets just obey the rules.

DJ Geespot

Yeah i have seen this issue on CNN and I'm sure the law will be passed sooner.I think in Iceland they've passed it already.

Mark

Mixmag in the UK recently conducted a survey among their readership, with 70 per cent agreeing that smoking should be banned in pubs and clubs—a much higher percentage than I'd have thought. There's an article on page 15 of the November issue, concerning Scottish government's plans to introduce a ban before the next election, and with England and Wales expected to follow suit—possibly as early as May 2005.
 It looks like the writing's on the wall!

Mark

Well, the shit has hit the fan on this one in Scotland, as you may have seen on the news this week, with a ban in public places now set to be implemented by Spring 2006. The Smoking Lobby have been bleating and moaning about the breach of their rights, but that's only to be expected.

Wales is now thought to be next in line, along with the city of Liverpool as the solitary spot in England, bizarrely. But it's surely only a matter of time before the government buckles under pressure with regard to the rest of England? I reckon a full UK ban will be in place within three years. Time for us in the clubland community to start thinking about how it's going to affect us!

Mark

OK, so the latest news sees the United Kingdom split on the issue. Scotland is going for a total ban, and Wales and Northern Ireland have yet to reveal their policies.

In England, it's a right shambles. A ban is now set to take place in licenced premises from 2006...but only where such places serve food. And then it'll probably only be partial! That means nightclubs won't be affected at all. On the one hand, no need to worry about a detrimental effect on business, with DJs losing their slots because venues can't afford to keep them on. On the other, we might still die of lung cancer before we're 50!

Mark

Came home smelling like an overflowing ashtray yet again last night. Clothes straight off and into the wash! In my opinion, a ban can't come soon enough!

**Don Juan
(Northampton, England)**

On a serious note, why all the fuss about smoking in clubs/pubs?

I never enjoy going home stinking of cigarettes, it's a nasty smell and doesn't exactly stir the oils of passion at then end of the night (if you know what I mean!). But isn't smoking is an inherent part of this side to society. People who don't like the smoky pub atmosphere don't go to smoky pubs.

And surely pubs/clubs supply what people want—if they'd got it wrong they'd soon be out of business right? Anyone who thinks it's that important to ban smoking in 'clubland' should put their hand in the pocket and open a venue based on these health conscious ethics. If it worked, this would have a much greater effect on the industry than legislation that the large majority are not sure whether they want or not. As is evident, the law makers can't even make up their mind so what we will end up with is a half arsed attempt that doesn't work anyway. Would offering people an alternative be more effective in changing the views of a population than trying to dictate to them what they can and can't do.

Probably said enough...

Peace.

Mark

Don, maybe your username should have been 'Devil's Advocate'??!

I rather suspect that if the Government didn't cream off so much from cigarette sales in tax, they wouldn't hesitate to impose a ban tomorrow. As it stands, it's currently a balancing act between how much it makes in tax on sales, and how much it costs the NHS to treat smoking-related diseases. Only Gordon Brown could tell you how the scales tip.

Don't think for a minute than anything like ethics and morals come into it. This is the Government we're talking about, after all!

Mark

Italy got in on the act this month, banning smoking in public places like bars and restaurants. And we all know the Italians like a fag!

It's happening, people!

Mark

Norway's been on board for quite a while, too, which I only just found out.

Mark

New Zealand, too, as I discovered on my recent visit. Australia's apparently next. No getting away from it, people—the revolution is happening!

Bee

Yes! Australia in 2007. I can't wait.

I'm a non smoker and hate being on dancefloors worrying that my clothes are going to get burnt. And I have 5 scars from Cigarette burns—I'll be popping the champagne when it's OUT!

Mark

Exactly! That's a point we've not discussed here yet! People carelessly waving their fags around while they're on the dancefloor.

Funnily enough, I got a burn to the arm when I was in Melbourne just the other week!

*

Mark Devlin

MICHAEL JACKSON: WHAT NOW?

Mark

It would be wrong to speculate too much on his guilt or otherwise while the trial still looms. But should a guilty verdict be delivered, will Jackson classics like 'Don't Stop Til You Get Enough' and 'Billie Jean' still be able to get played to the same degree of enthusiasm as before? Remember Gary Glitter? You don't hear a single one his records on the
 radio since his conviction. (OK, they were crap...) Is Michael destined for the same? Or will great music always be great music, regardless of the private life of the creator?

Belfast's Finest

Funny enough, I was DJing in a bar a few nights after the allegations were released, and this girl came up and bitched at me for playing 'You rock my world', saying that he was a an evil bastard and that wouldn't I look stupid for ever playing his music...

To me, music is music, and when Michael is at his best, music is at it's best. No matter what he does in his private life, his music is still outstanding.

Mark

I would have to agree. Remember, James Brown and Rick James were woman-beaters, but no-one has a problem with their records being played.

It's just some sad, sad shit to see what Michael has become. He used to be a truly legendary and hugely influential figure in black music. Now, he's just a joke. And even if he's cleared of all charges, will anyone's view of him ever be the same again?

Sad indeed.

DJ Geespot

Well I just remember watching Chris Rock's Never Scared when he said we love Michael Jackson so much that we let the first child slip... Well I'm not sure if people will still love him like they used to even if he can be acquitted of the charges. Well James Brown was abuse wa on people who could make decisive decisions but Michael's case on children in totally ridiculous. I'm not surprised that he is a laughing stock, coz he has done the unexcusable. And twice for that matter..

Mark

Interesting that nobody seems to getting that upset about R Kelly's allegations, and continues to happily blaze his tracks. Let's not forget that, like MJ, he stands accused, (but as yet unconvicted), of alleged sex with minors. Is the difference that R's (alleged—let's keep this legal!) encounters are with little girls, whereas Michael's are—allegedly -with little boys? Does that make the idea more acceptable somehow?

Or is it just that R is still at the peak of his career and making great tunes, whereas Wacko dried up years ago??

Mark

Yeah—this one could run and run. Let's keep this topic open!

Don Juan

Mark—valid comment ref: R Kelly.

Personally, I don't think it's so much the difference between little boys and girls. I propose 2 theories.,

1. R Kelly is big in the Urban world whereas MJ is big in the whole world. The billions of extra people with an interest in this case means the media has stepped up its involvement so now everyone has an opinion.

2. The US feel they let him slip last time (rightly or wrongly) and some Americans wont forgive them for that. They're making sure this time they go all out for a guilty verdict and if he proves his innocence, then at least they tried.

Me—it's all about the music. If people can't differentiate the two then they need to sort it out.

Mark

I just don't understand the Americans. They build up MJ to a global superstar, then they want nothing more than to see him brought down.

Meanwhile, George W Bush cheats his way into office, lies to the American public, and creates the biggest threat to world peace the modern world has ever seen...so they vote him in for a second term.

Hello...??

DJ Geespot

Good to hear that the king of pop's jury selection process is continuing after the short spell of flu.Its said there is a paraplegic and an older woman who are still to be interviewed, or is it an interview.You can never understand the Americans. But I think most of the time its because they only have information about their country and dont know a single thing about the rest of the world.

They think when you get off an airplane in Africa you'll see lions and elephants walking outside the airstrip,coz thats what they see in national geographic special,animals in Africa. That's why they believe everything that Bush says,and they dont care about civilian casualities in Iraq coz they never see those kind of news.And they think if they want to take down MJ why must they not do it.SO it will be interesting to see what happens.His music I'm sure it'll live on,the question is how sure,or rather how long?

Mark

It's all hotting up again now. The next few weeks should make some interesting news-watching.

Mark

Oh dear. Turning up to court an hour late in pyjamas and slippers and narrowly avoiding a warrant for arrest is not the way to win the public's support, Michael!

My opinion on this whole subject veers from considering the whole trial to be a witch hunt by greedy unscrupulous goldiggers one minute, to reluctantly conceding that Michael has become just the kind of loopy fruitcake that really could have done it the next.

I just don't know.

Mark

I'm actually starting to feel quite sorry for the dude now.

Try this—hold up a copy of the sleeve to 'Off The Wall' or 'Thriller'. Then compare the face you see with the latest picture of MJ from the papers.

Says it all, really.

DJ Hix

it's a terrible shame that such a talent has turned out like this. i consider myself an enormous fan, always have been, but as a performer only. unfortunately his utter naivety has landed him in this "no way out" situation.

even if he is innocent (which i still hope he is), it's hard to see how he could come back from this.

if his private life wasn't so disturbing and irregular that it didn't over-shadow his talents, he would surely go on for years.

Think about it. Michael Jackson would undoubtedly be remembered as the greatest entertainer that ever lived.

now, its so sad that he'll more than likely be remembered as the most tragic downfall in history.

Mark

Yeah. The average artist would have spotted Bashir's motives a mile off and realised that you DO NOT, under any circumstances, admit on TV to having young boys in your bedroom!

Lee

He will get convicted, the evidence this week will nail him. From what I have heard and seen on the web and watching the Court case replays on Sky One I think he will get convicted, and he will be chucked off the radio.

Mark

So, MJ got off! A victory for justice, or further proof that no black celebrity will EVER go to jail?! (OJ? Guilty as hell, but free as a bird!)

R Kelly's next to be let off the hook. Just watch.

I'm happy that Wacko didn't get locked down, as I doubt he would have survived jail. It still leaves the question of what the hell he was going to do for the rest of his life, though. His career's not exactly at its strongest right now!

Last edited by Mark on Wed Jun 22, 2005 12:01 pm; edited 1 time in total

Mark

Oh yeah, I forgot. Michael's not the only one whose career's fucked.
Martin Bashir, anyone?!

Mark

Just to quantify my earlier remark that no black celebrity ever goes to jail, what I meant was no black MAINSTREAM celebrity, (OJ, MJ, etc) This ruling does not, of course, apply to rappers. I won't begin to list the number of MCs that have spent time on lockdown, as I doubt there's space on this forum's server!
Happily, I'd consider R Kelly to now have crossed over into the mainstream category. (Membership of this is loosely based around whether my Mum has actually heard of the celeb in question.)

Mark

There's now strong talk of MJ's people trying to rush out a new comeback album before the end of the year!

*

Mark Devlin

DISS RECORDS—DO WE NEED THEM?

Mark

Diss records have become a staple part of current hip hop output. The newest one to throw fuel on the fire is 50 Cent's 'Piggy Bank', where he subliminally disses Xzibit, Jadakiss, Fat Joe, Nas and others. This has already prompted a vicious answer-back from Fat Joe, and a joint one between Joe and Jadakiss.

Do diss records bring excitement and energy to the game? Are they dangerous? (would 2Pac still be alive if he hadn't released 'Hit 'Em Up'?) Lyrical battle exchanges and 'Ya Mama' jokes are one thing, but when things start moving on to gun talk, is this something we really want our music to be associated with?

It's not just a US thing now, either. In the UK grime/hip hop scene, little beefs are starting to spring up. The latest is between Roll Deep and Wiley, and prior to that, Crazy Titch and Dizzee Rascal had a thing going, where Titch switched up Dizzee's 'he's just a rascal, a Dizzee Rascal' lyric to 'you're just an arsehole, a silly arsehole.'

Do you ever get the feeling these UK dudes are watching how the Americans do it and inventing their own beefs for the sake of controversy?

Or are they just boring, and no substitute for real creativity? Does 50 Cent calling Fat Joe 'that fat nigga' really speak to you and inspire you in your life?

DJ Geespot

I think all these diss tracks are just there to attract attention. I mean, I'm sitting here talking about them now, right?!

Tales from the Flipside

I think artists make them to push sales and to get interviews and magazine covers faster, in the hope that consumers then rush to buy the album to hear what they're saying about whom, then anxiously wait for the response.

Mark

There's a possibility that there's no real beef there. They're all friends that have agreed to create a situation that helps sell records for al of them.

Anyone peeped the Jadakiss answer-back to 50's 'Piggy Bank' yet? It's vicious!

DJ Geespot

I'm kinda getting bored with it all now. There's yet another reply from 50 Cent and Tony Yayo saying 'I run New York' for Jadakiss and Fat Joe. Please, guys—we need some real lyrical talent now.

Mark

It all reminds me of schoolyard name-calling, like the last one to speak has somehow won the game.

DJ Riddler

Don't get me wrong. I like diss records. Nas' 'Ether' is one of the best tracks ever. So was 'Hit 'Em Up'.

But too many rappers are now at each others' throats. Jadakiss is lyrically sick; he doesn't even need to stoop so low as to respond to 50 Cent. And as for Fat Joe—he's gangsta. Why would anyone really want to fuck with him?!

Basically, I think we should all stop buying 50's albums and try to recreate the good old days of just spitting your 16 bars and getting paid.

Mark

Wouldn't it be entertaining if R&B artists took hip hop's lead and started putting out diss records? Imagine R Kelly crooning insults at Usher.

Or even pop artists. Picture Elton John at his piano bitching away about George Michael!

*

RAVES FROM THE GRAVE—IS IT WRONG?

Mark

December sees the release of a full album of Biggie Smalls tracks on Bad Boy. It'll merge Biggie vocals from the archive with new input from various artists, and entirely new production. You know the format—they've been doing it with 2Pac for years! The first single is 'Hold Your Head' which merges Biggie's vocals with Bob Marley's, produced by Clinton Sparks.

The album will probably be incredible to listen to, and a real treat for fans. But is there a moral aspect to it? Is it right to continually capitalise on the deaths of Biggie, 2Pac and everyone else—particularly on the Biggie 'n' Bob joint? The families of the artists will get some of the money, but it's the record execs who'll make the most dough!

Or is this just over-reacting, and should we just enjoy the music and not get so uptight?!

Lee

I can't stand the way they are bringing out a new 2pac album every 6 months...Its the only way his mum and Death Row can make money!

And now Death Row or is it the "Tha Row?" have just released another Greatest Hits of the old classics from Dre, 2pac and Snoop...its like their 200th Greatest Hits from the now "we have no great artists please buy our re-released albums!"

The Biggie thing is just another way of Puffy/P-Diddy/Diddy/ or Just plain P to get money (not that he needs it) leave the dead artist how they were and lets remember them for the tracks that they did when they were alive...

Please Mr Eminem...put down the 2pac album...no remixes here!

DJ Puffy
(Oxford, England)

Don't be too shocked to find a Jam Master Jay greatest mixes in the shops soon

Molf

I think the death of an artist should not be the end of everything,his legacy should remain behind,something which will make us neva forget that there was once an artist called xxx,but what i have some problem with is the quality of that music,for sure it wont b` like if it wasn't him in that real sense. I do support the release of these albums because some of them they played a very big role by then on the music industry.

DJ Geespot

Yeah I'm feeling everybody on this one and I think its time this record labels start hunting for some talent that is great so that we can hear some new tunes now.I mean some of the collaborations on the new 2 pac albums sometimes make me wonder if 2 pac would have collaborated with those artists. And also some of the unreleased material that always surface I think had a reason not to be released.It was wack back then it is still wack now.

Remember Tupac sang changes,"thats just the way it is,things will never be the same".SO people must learn to move on, and give us some new material,and I'm not talking about remixes or old lyrics blended on new instrumentals.I'm sure it'll get to a point when they have no more greatest hits,but be sure to get the greatest of greatest hits album.Please they were great then now lest get the great staff now.Lets move on...I'm not saying lets not play the old staff or not buy it, but it should be once in a while...

Mark

True. Can you see Tupac going into a studio with Elton John? It would never have happened!

What next? Big L and Cliff Richard?

*

ELECT YOUR FORGOTTEN CLASSICS

Mark

Zane Lowe has a feature on his Radio 1 show named 'Rockets From The Crypt'. It's where listeners suggest favourite tracks that never made it big, but should have done. Specifically, this refers to album tracks, B-sides, bootlegs, soundtrack tunes...anything that wasn't a big hit, but which still sounds great nevertheless.

To get the ball rolling, I'd have to put forward 'Don't Curse', a posse cut that appeared on Heavy D & The Boyz'

'Peaceful Journey' album in 1991. It features Grand Puba, Q Tip, Pete Rock, CL Smooth, Big Daddy Kane each taking a verse, and it's an absolute classic. You never hear it played anywhere, though.

Other suggestions...?

Karl Cross

Tune Mark!
 also used to love Nice n Smooths—Down The Line!
 How about some EPMD? Boon Dox or Cant Here Nothin but the music!

Mark

Da Brat and Biggie's 'Da B Side' from about 1994 is another one. I've only ever heard one other DJ play that in the UK. It's an absolute masterpiece!

Belfast's Finest

Biggie & Method Man—The What. I always loved this joint...
 ATCQ—oh my god...

Mark

True. And on the subject of Wu Tang, Ol' D B's under-exposed 'Brooklyn Zoo' really should be the track everyone remembers him for, rather than the pop moment that is 'Got Your Money.'

Mark

Anyone remember Naughty By Nature's 'Mourn You Til I Join You', their tribute to 2Pac from 1997? I just heard it on a tape of one of my old radio shows, and damn, it still sounds good!

Mark

Just remembered Ed OG & The Bulldogs 'I Got Ta Have It' too. The beat was last heard on Mary J Blige's 'Oooh' from her 2003 album. Classic.

Mark

Main Source have to be the all-time much-forgotten hip hop crew. Nobody mentions them now, or ever plays their joints. But anyone remember just how hot the likes of 'Looking At The Front Door', 'Live at the BBQ' and 'Fakin' The Funk' were in the early 90s? Now, that's REAL music!

Mark

Heard Deee-Lite's 'Groove Is In The Heart' up in a club last night. Although a well-known pop hit, it's ages since I've heard it—and damn, it sounded good! If it's good enough for Q-Tip, it's good enough for me!

Karl Cross

Yeah Mark,
  Main Source were the Bome as were label mates...
  UMC's, One To Grow On, Blue Cheese.
  Brand Nubian... Slow Down and later Punks Jump up (minus Puba)
  Das EFX—Mic Checka (Remix) That Bassline & intro was like Whoa!
  Lost Boyz—Jeeps & Rene

Naughty By Nature—Uptown Anthem
Big Daddy Kane—Wrath Of Kane

Belfast's Finest

Crooklyn Dodgers—Crooklyn Anthem
Brand Nubian—Punks Jump up...(so good I'll echo it!!)
Redman—Tonight's da night
And lately
Horace Brown—Shake it up
Ideal—Whatever

UK VIP Pimp

why are there only hip-hop tracks in your oldies debate?
D'angelo—Lady
mtume—juicy...
PAUSE!!!!
dont get me started. the only way i get to hear these in a club is is if i play them myself!!!!

Mark

Mtume? Standard!
There are only hip tracks cos that's what people have been nominating, but I'm more than happy to get some classic soul/ R&B tunes jumping off here.

Mark

On the dancehall front, anyone remember Patra's 'Romantic Call' from about 1994? Classic. Might have to dig it out and start slipping it into my sets again!

Mark

Raphael Saadiq and Q Tip's 'Get Involved' seems to have become a bit of a revered classic among hip hop DJs. I heard Blakey cutting it up on Radio 1/ 1Xtra recently, and it's just cropped up on a DJ Skully/ IQ mix CD.

I've always loved this. It's a classic party tune with a totally infectious beat.

*

ROCKETS FROM THE CRYPT

DJ Geespot

Well I'm not sure if its really forgotten but A tribe Called Quest's—Find a Way. I always hear people playing 'I c u doing it' ...

D-NO

Eric Benet—Georgy Porgy
 Platinum Pied Pipers—Open your eyes (and the original too)
 Jazzy Jeff—For tha love of da game

JoeBoy

How about Derrick Dimitri—Get it on tonight?

Mark

Good one. Forget the Montell Jordan cover!

Guest

Why did Montell's make it so big when its just basically exact same?

Mark

Nothing's fair in the music game!

Lee

The Roots—Proceed III(Feat. Bahamadia)
Love this track...can't find it anywhere...

Mark

Oh yeah, and remember Bahamadia 'Uknowhowwedu'? I still play that now sometimes.

*

TOP 10 ALBUMS—YOUR INPUT NEEDED!

Mark

To mark the 50th anniversary of the official UK album charts this year, the people at The Guinness World Records are compiling an All-Time Favourite Album chart based on votes by members of the British public.

This is too good an opportunity to miss. To be a part of it and make sure your favourite sets get included, just e-mail your top ten (Number/ artist/ title) to James.Bradley@guinnessworldrecords.com. It's as simple as that.

It would also be good if people could post their votes up here as well, so we can get a feel for what people are saying. For the record, here are mine. Yeah, of course there's a few unexpected ones in there—that's what these lists are all about, isn't it?!

1. SNOOP DOGGY DOGG: DOGGY STYLE (1993)
2. PRINCE: PURPLE RAIN (1984)
3. MICHAEL JACKSON: THRILLER (1982)
4. DR. DRE: THE CHRONIC (1992)
5. NOTORIOUS B.I.G: READY TO DIE (1994)
6. JERU THA DAMAJA: WRATH OF THE MATH (1996)
7. BEE GEES: SATURDAY NIGHT FEVER O.S.T (1977)
8. HUMAN LEAGUE: DARE (1981)
9. MIKE OLDFIELD: TUBULAR BELLS (1973)
10. A TRIBE CALLED QUEST: MIDNIGHT MARAUDERS (1993)

DJ Geespot

As a young person I'm sure my All-Time Favourite will not be that old, but here it goes

1. Nas—Ill Matic
2. Snoop—Doggy Style
3. Jay Z—Reasonable Doubt
4. Dr Dre—Chronic
5. Boogie Down Productions-Criminal Minded
6. Slick Rick—The Great Adventures of Slick Rick
7. NWA—N*ggaz 4 life
8. Run-DMC—Raising Hell
9. 2 Pac—The Don Killuminati
10. Notorious BIG—Ready To Die

I believe save the best for the last and i'm a big fan of Biggie,but then my friend likes Tu Pac though I'm not his biggest fan

Mark

That's a pretty classic selection.

DJ Geespot

I had to be classic...And its only now that I realised that I love hip hop so much that I didn't include albums from other music genres..But anyway you said 'based on votes by members of the British public. ' so I won't make that much of difference...

DJ Hix

dunno about my top10, that may take a bit of thinking...
but number one for me?
Michael Jackson—Off The Wall
sounds incredible no matter how many times I play it.
he's a freak, but in my books he's the greatest performer thats ever lived.

Mark

Word up.

Lee

1. Prince—Purple Rain /O-l-> Album/ Diamonds and Pearls
2. 2pac—All Eyez on Me
3. Eminem—Slim Shaddy LP
4. Snoop Dogg-Doggy Style

5. Q-Tip—Amplified
6. Dr Dre—Tha Chronic / Tha Chronic II
7. Mos Def—Black on Both Sides
8. Redman/Method Man—Tha Blackout
9. Ice Cube Album—The Predator

One of Busta Rhymes...not sure which one...I'll try greatest hits!

This is hard where do I put Biggie and NWA??? and Beyonce and the Fugees? ????

Mark

I forgot to include Eminem's Slim Shady LP in mine. A true landmark album. It's easy to forget the impact this had when it first dropped. We're used to Eminem now, but back then, nobody had heard anything quite like this!

Bee

It's so hard to do lists like this as I get bored too easy
 In the top ten though, I'd definitely have to have:
 Red Hot Chili Peppers—Blood Sugar Sex Magik

*

UNSUNG HEROES—DJs WHO REALLY DESERVE THE PROPS

Mark

This one's similar to the Rockets From The Crypt thread, in the Tuneage section. There, we want your forgotten classic tunes. Here, we're looking for nominations for the post of Most Under-rated DJ—you know, that really hot dude or dudette that's miles ahead of the so-called market leaders in turntable skills, crowd-rocking ability, and overall performance.

To get the ball rolling, my nomination goes to Danny Drastic outta New York City. I gotta be honest; it's not often I witness another DJ who totally stops me in my tracks, but this guy's set at Avalon in Manhattan this month was awesome. He managed to show some mad turntable trickery, but without ever losing the bounce and flow of the set, which is a combination not many DJs achieve. We recorded the set, and it'll be posted on the site for all to hear very soon.

Nominate your own Unsung Heroes here...

Belfast's Finest

Oh this is easy—DJ Kofi from London. That guy is frighteningly good. He's much better than Shortee, but doesn't seem to have ever broken through, which is a shame as he's a great bloke as well.

Mark

True dat. I caught Kofi at Thompsons in Belfast a couple of years ago, and he was absolutely incredible. I stood there watching him with my jaw open, feeling like a fan. Almost embarrassing.

Sam Young

I agree, Kofi is the dogs bollocks when it comes to djing,heavy skills and he drops in the odd tune you wouldn't expect to hear. also, my boy Harry Love used to be in the scratch perverts, heavy producer and hiphop DJ. he just did some cuts for blak twang.

and stateside this guy called jus ske, not as big as flex and clue etc, but he does all the hot parties and he can mix it up real nice.

Belfast's Finest

Location: Belfast

I was wondering were Harry Love had come from; he makes some hot joints.

Guest

He's from London. I think he was a one-time Scratch Pervert. Now does stuff on his own. He's never had a particularly high profile, but he's revered in underground circles.

Mark

DJ Matchstick, who runs the Warner Street Team is kinda nice on the decks. Caught him blazing it at The Brunel Rooms in Swindon recently.

Many other DJs will surely agree—they want to retain their place on his mailing list!

Mark

Hardly under-rated, but having been mesmerised by Jazzy Jeff's performance in Reading last night, (a two-hour set using Final Scratch,) it would be a very serious mmission not to include the guy here. Many consider him to be the greatest DJ in the world, which he might just be...

Mark

I received a mixtape CD recently from a dude called DJ Smasherelly outta London. First time I've come across him. His blending, scratching, track selection and flow were all kinda tight.

Anyone else know this guy?

Mark

DJ Classic outta San Francisco deserves props here. A real main player of the US West Coast scene—hot clubs, mixtapes, productions, remixes, etc. Remember the name

D-NO

DJ Pogo and DJ Kofi.

Mark

Haven't heard anything from DJ Pogo since the 80s! I know Kofi's still destroying things, tho'!

Lee

DJ Lil Chris...
 But I'm biased because I do his website!
 http://www.djlilchris.com

*

HOW CHAV IS YOUR HOOD?

Mark

The Chavs are taking over! It's knocked-off fake Burberry and Ralph Lauren everywhere. And a curry and a fight on the way home. I need to know the regions where the Chavs are repping the strongest right now.

Personally, I'd have to nominate my hometown of Bicester. I mean, have you ever seen outside G's on a Thursday night? And as far as Chav anthems go, that's easy—Ice Cube's 'You Can Do It' and Khia's 'My Neck My Back' every time!

Belfast's Finest

We have our regional variation—The 'Spide'
Look up Spide in http://www.urbandictionary.com
As we also have the harshest accents in the UK, you can imagine what these beauts are like.

Lee

The 'Spide' sounds like the same thing!
Love the urbandictionary!

Mark

Let's not forget the Pikeys, who preceded the Chavs by several generations!

UK VIP Pimp

Now in my opinion, it's either Liverpool or my home town of Stoke-on-Trent who are the originators of Chavmanship!!! with exception of Pikey's of course

Mark

Were the Harry Enfield 'calm down' permed-head characters very early incarnations of Chavs then? I guess they were.

Mark

I think we should assemble a Top Ten of Chav Tunes. Alongside obvious entries like The Streets and Goldie Looking Chain, Ice Cube's 'You Can Do It' would have to be in there. The number one spot must surely go to Khia's 'My Neck My Back'. It really is getting depressing having to watch crusty council estate girls singing the lyrics and thinking they're sexy. No! It's wrong!

Ciara's 'Goodies' seems to be going the same way. It's a shame. cos it's still a hot tune.

Chippie

I think chav's are great...a real british trend...and because of films like snatch and lock stock.. we are gonna get a lot more...

Belfast's Finest

Is it me, or do any of the rest of the lads here find council estate girls in pink velour tracksuits a total turn-on??? They just look so derrrrty; so wrong yet so right...

So it's just me then...

Mark

I think that viewpoint depends on how long it is since you last got served!

Mark

The Game 'How We Do' seems to becoming a new Chav anthem. Not a good look.

Karl Cross

Anything by Nelly!?

Belfast's Finest

I had to get my mum a CD for Mother's Day, so went to the closest town with an HMV to her—Bangor (Northern Ireland), a Max Power endorsed town, no less .

This is the Chav capital—souped up shitbox cars, burberry caps, spotty birds with lots of jewellery; I was astonished that the music of choice blasting out of the speakers; instead of questionable trance anthems, was Westwood-style joints (Ciara, the Game, Fiddy)

It's official—the scene is fucked...

Mark

Westwood seems to be openly recruiting Chavs as fans lately. (Just take a look at the Photo Gallery on his website for proof—www.timwestwood.com) Clearly, it's his latest bid to remain popular with the masses and retain his position. The spin-off effect on the music and the scene was inevitable.

Mark

Another new Chav anthem is 'Ladies' by The Crooklyn Clan. Although I've been playing it virtually every weekend since 1997, I'm now getting asked for 'that new Ladies' tune' in many places I play. It's 'Be Faithful' all over again.

I find it very sad when what started out as a quality credible tune makes the cross-over into mindless mainstream fodder territory.

Belfast's Finest

That's Def Jam's fault for raping & pillaging AV8's back catalogue for a cheap buck. 'Franklinz' will be next.

Mind you, it was good putting 'Be Faithful' away—6 years is an awful long time to hear a track EVERY time you go out.

www.ingramcontent.com/pod-product-compliance
Lightning Source LLC
Chambersburg PA
CBHW011957090526
44590CB00023B/3752